THE ELECTRICIAN'S CHILDREN

How one Irish family took Jesus' conspiracy of hope across the globe

by David Wilson

with Pam Wilson, Myles Wilson and Ruth McNeill

Published by Agapé Ireland
March 2023

ISBN 978-0-9565814-3-3
Agapé Ireland
Ulysses House
22-24 Foley Street
Dublin
D01 W2T2
www.agape.ie
office@agape.ie

Cover design: Joel Wilson

Printed by
Ross Print Services, Greystones, Co. Wicklow
www.rossprint.ie

ACKNOWLEDGEMENTS

This book describes our family's experience of promoting Jesus in the various circumstances of our lives.

In so doing, we have lifted the lid off some rare views such as Irish rural life in all its remoteness in the 1920s, inside the Plymouth Brethren in the later twentieth century, and the inside view of the missionary life of a family spread across the world, many serving with the Agapé movement. We realise that our perspective is our own. We also realise that these inside views may appear unfamiliar. But this is what we saw. We were there. A string of fellow-travellers egged us on to write it all down - you know who you are.

We are very grateful to our publishing friends at Agapé for supplying editorial expertise and good old moral support. Thank you too to Joel Wilson for coming up with both the title and the cover image – and to Ross Print Services for the book design work.

My wife Pam is listed as a co-author but she is much more than that – she's my best friend and my adventurous companion.

Our family tree has also been enriched by missionaries like Helen and Gerald Clarke, Edith Clarke, Liam Burns, Lyn and Andrew Griffin, Joel and Danielle Wilson, Lorna and Stephen McGowan, Joyce and David Swan and others. They have served on five continents. It's a big tree. You have to keep a close eye on it because you never know who'll move next. We have confined our story to the branch we know best.

Many on that tree are not mentioned here. I am sure that they live perfectly normal, productive lives. Although, don't quote me on that!

This aptly titled book *The Electrician's Children* is first and foremost charged with a selfless commitment to the Scriptures.

David Wilson's account of three generations of his family and their love and conviction of the Bible as an essential element in peoples finding Christ is a story that will inspire any reader who hungers for God's Word as well as the reader whose appetite is yet to be whetted.

David, his wife Pam and his siblings were so imbued with biblical faith that they easily influenced others and in time it grew into a worldwide movement. The reader will be left at once mesmerised by the extent of their work as well as being inspired by their example.

I have no doubt that this book is not only a testament to their work but will also serve as an inspired instrument to bring many to commit to Jesus of the Bible.

Sr Marie McNamara - *Former Principal of Spanish Point Secondary School*

This book is the incredible story of a remarkable family. An ordinary family with mission in their veins. This is the story of disarming courage, indescribable generosity and heartrending personal suffering. A captivating Christ-centred global vision has gripped their souls. In burnout and breaking out their dependence on God is life changing. Boredom is non-existent. A passion for making disciples and obeying Christ pervades every part of their lives and lifestyles. . . You will be inspired, encouraged and moved by reading this book. I certainly have!

Rt. Rev. Kenneth Clarke - *Former Bishop of Kilmore, Elphin and Ardagh*

David Wilson's account of his family's missionary story is very readable, often moving and also, at times, funny. His book shows us God's grace in action across the years. The electrician from Derry and his wife from rural Donegal were generous to God. But not without return. Through them, God raised up three missionaries and filled their lives with joyful service. There are many truths to be learned in these pages. One is that good parents are a blessing not just to their own children but to the whole world. Another is that, no matter how strange the times may seem to us, God will raise up people, and sometimes in the most surprising of places, to do his work.

'There's nothing like the company of people who will discuss the big issues of life together', writes David Wilson. This book, and the people it depicts, are great company themselves. And, as the writer makes clear, Christ is the best company of all.

Senator Rónán Mullen - *Member of the Irish Senate*

CONTENTS

CHAPTER ONE

BREESY MOUNTAIN

Saturday night in Derry during the Second World War was a sight to behold. Mainly because there was nothing to behold at all. It was under strict Blackout laws - not a chink of light to be seen. That didn't stop Guildhall Square filling up with all the girls and guys trying to get in touch with each other. Including Annie Myles and her new beau, Joe Wilson, whom she had met on her first day in town. The enterprising Joe had found a way to make his presence known amongst all the various voices in the multitude. He whistled. And not just any old whistle. He whistled the hymn 'It is well with my soul'.

It was almost like a bird call which invariably produced Annie by his side. She had met him on her first day in town as he was selling little lapel badges to raise money for the St John Ambulance Brigade who, in those days, spent a lot of their time tending to casualties of air-raids. Joe always dressed smartly without looking unnecessarily dapper. His dark hair suited the growing of a moustache which he had originally acquired when, as a young electrician working in the shipyard in Belfast, he was made foreman and needed to assert his authority.

I doubt if Joe had learned about Annie's family background at the level of detail we now know. But he knew this much – it was her soul that captured his attention. And he knew about the fateful decision she had made just before he met her. Joe's city-boy life could scarcely have been further from Annie's amazing upbringing, despite being less than 70 miles away. Annie herself didn't consider it amazing while she was growing up (what child begins by thinking, 'My life is amazing'?!). It was only as seasoned adults that my mother, Annie, and her siblings realised what a remarkable start life had given them, especially when one of them, Molly, died at the age of 66.

The siblings fell into the habit of returning, every July, to the old birthplace. In a certain sense it was Molly who drew them together more closely this time because her sister, my Aunt Bessie, had come up with a way in which the surviving siblings could hold on to their past. Bessie had been a teacher in Greencastle in north Donegal and her amazingly effective primary-school-type proposal was for everyone to take a simple little notebook and write down their memories of the 1920s and 30s. She wasn't asking them to do it right there on the day (she was cannier than that). The plan was that they would write for a year and come back to the same spot in 12 months.

On that return visit the siblings chatted amiably, with the odd glance out of the window at the changeable weather. Had the weather been clearer they would have been able to see the top of Breesy mountain on which their lone caravan was permanently parked. Had they climbed to the top of Breesy (which they often did in mid-July) they could have seen five counties from there – Tyrone, Fermanagh, Leitrim, Sligo and of course their own Donegal. Five counties on the horizon – but there wasn't much human habitation to be found on that mountain. There never had been.

All of them were in their seventies now, except Jim who was almost seventy – and he was the one who had parked the caravan there in recent years just so they would still have a foothold on the mountain.

On my desk I have my mother's notebook from that one-year reunion. She was Molly's other sister. You can feel the granular detail of an eyewitness in her notes. Her record of daily life includes:

'Mother often washed the clothes in Fermanagh and dried them in Donegal! They were rinsed in the river (that was the dividing line) and that saved carrying rinsing-water – then in good weather she spread them out on the Donegal side to dry. Blanket washing was a big job. They were washed outside, in a big tub, and we got our turn at tramping them with our bare feet. At least our feet were clean afterwards.'

That entry in her journal gives a sneak preview into the family's life in the 1920s, on a tiny farm perched on the border between Northern Ireland and what was then the Irish Free State. Now in her seventies, she was reading it out loud to four of her siblings, poised sedately on bench seats in a caravan jut one field away from that same river.

Sibling John was also in attendance that day. He had been famous among us for years as Mr Taciturn. He didn't have a bad word to say, let me stress. It's just that he seldom had any word to say at all. Somehow the notebook allowed him to take flight and he became veritably verbose – if not in speech, at least in writing.

He expounded further on the vast range of country skills practised by the family, like plaiting hay into rope and making bee skeps (who knew?!) and yes, I have to keep a dictionary handy when I read the now loquacious John Myles. He and his wife Joie eventually transformed his notes into a handmade hardback book. You almost knew it was going to be handmade, like everything else.

Interruptions to life on a quiet rural Donegal hill farm creep in here and there. John records that he and his friend Joe Mulhern listened to the ordnance disposal unit dealing with the bombs jettisoned by a Sunderland flying-boat which crash-landed in the Cashelard bog in August 1944. I'd never heard of such a thing! He informs us that it came down 'in bogland near Deveneys' home'. Now we know! Somebody recently asked me, 'Have you checked that on Google?' Why should I? Uncle John was obviously there and Google obviously wasn't.

The whole story tumbles out through the notes of the siblings who have, at that point, weathered seventy years. For me, it's like reading an Enid Blyton 'Famous Five' adventure book for children and finding out that it was all true and that your mother was one of them.

Their father, Robert Myles, was born in 1859, ten years after the Famine, and had emigrated to the United States, back when there weren't quite so many states in the union. After seven years in Philadelphia he changed his mind, returned to County Donegal and at the age of 60 married my grandmother, the 22-year-old Helen Stevenson. She first set eyes on him at Ballintra cattle mart and apparently that was enough to melt her heart (she was on a summer holiday from Glasgow!). They set up home beside Breesy mountain in a three-room thatched cottage (no running water, bathroom, toilet, ceilings or flooring) and Helen bore him six children, three girls and three boys, in fairly rapid succession. He soon died, while most of the children were still at home, and she set forth on the considerable work of bringing up the six – Molly, Annie (my mother), Bertie, Bessie, John and Jim.

But the six remembered their Breesy start in life as a mostly care-free adventure. John, and the others, chronicle a childhood full of wonder at the natural world. They were almost spellbound by the making of hay (which I had always imagined to be a tedious chore). In fact they wrote that, 'Haystack day was the highlight of the season.' Mowing was done by scythe and as Bessie remembered that skilful work she saw 'the rhythm in it was soothing to watch and almost poetic.'

Mowing was only the start. People then worked in twos to make grasscocks (small piles of hay) before the main event – the making of the hayrick. This would be their specially constructed pile of hay to see them through the winter. This required your classical Irish *meitheal* - a farm working party made up of all the neighbours from miles around who could volunteer for the day. A lot of tea was drunk and even cake was eaten.

To firm up the rick it needed to be tramped down on the top – a job that the children gladly volunteered for. There followed a health and safety nightmare as the happy siblings jumped up and down on the rick while men were feeding more and more hay on to it with pitchforks. Everybody survived that exercise. The only visible wounds were tiny insect bites of midges and clegs, the infamous enemies of hay making, which were held at bay by smearing the children's arms and legs with Vaseline so the insects would stick to them instead of bite.

Not every single blade of hay went into the rick. Some was kept to make ropes (again, in my imagination I thought you just bought ropes in rope shops). All it needed was an armful of well-chosen hay and 'twisters' – a hand crafted tool made from a wooden handle and a piece of strong wire. The hay was placed in a corner of the kitchen by the fire where Myles Snr took his seat and one of the kids took the twisters. He put a little loop of hay over the crook and the rope-making began as he fed the twisters. The person with the twisters would walk backwards to the end of the kitchen, through the bedroom door to the far end of that room when the new length was spliced on to a growing ball of rope. The whole show was a family production.

Each member of the family was likewise a part of threshing their crop of oats – with another set of wooden implements. Everybody took a hand with the cows. 'I didn't milk until I was nine,' my mother writes, 'In the winter I held the lamp – an easier job.' That's the point in the story where I realised they were milking in the dark! The inseparable Molly and Annie were carrying bags of turf from the bog one day when they saw their first aeroplane. They dropped the turf and ran home because they reckoned that if the plane fell out of the sky it would cover all their fields.

The siblings' notes make these surrounding fields sound like a wonderland. John lists four lakes that he and Bertie fished in. I can't even find them on an ordnance survey map. When they heard in school about the cuckoo's wily way of hijacking other birds' nests, they were delighted to verify every stage of the process with a nest in their own field. It was a world occupied not just by them but by those with which they shared the countryside – from the wren to the nightjar, corncrake, wild geese and snipe.

Bessie was acknowledged as the best at fishing but her forte was teaching. As a little child she would line up the others and 'teach' them. Like most of the others she didn't actually start school until she was seven because it was three miles away. That was three miles up the road – a road constructed by Robert Myles and his brothers but poorly maintained by Donegal County Council. Her day arrived. Here's how she put it:

'Previously, my known world did not go beyond the skyline of that valley which, in itself, offered many learning opportunities. The slow pace of life gave time for studying unknowingly, the wonders of nature – the changing seasons, the phases of the moon, daylight and darkness, plant life, insect life, bird life and animal life. There was plenty to arouse wonder and provoke thought. One did not have to be a scientist or even an adult to appreciate nature. What counted was seeing, touching and feeling, smelling, hearing and sometimes tasting and surviving!'

The eventual arrival at Upper Carricknahorna National School was a heart-pounding moment for Bessie. 'Feeling very backward and shy, I walked towards the door and removed the beret by catching the tassel and lifting it slowly above my head…I was a big girl now and my world was expanding.' It was the entry into an expanded world where she would spend the rest of her life. Her fervent pursuit of knowledge apparently knew no bounds. Once she secretly wrote on a scrap of paper her vow to 'work hard at my lessons' which she then burned 'before anyone came in'…'To me it was an almost sacred act, somewhat like "taking the pledge" '.

Bessie could write her name 'in joined writing' before she even went to school – because she was opening a post office savings account. One winter day the snow was so deep that she had to find her way to school by guesswork. The only other person who turned up was the teacher who gave her a reward she remembered seventy years later – a blood orange. She had never seen one before.

All the Myles children went to school barefoot for most of the year. For years I thought this was horrendous until I read Bessie's cheery account: 'In general, we looked forward to the "barefoot" season, provided it didn't begin too soon, due to boots having gone past the mending stage or feet having grown too big. While the frosty mornings were still with us and the feet still soft, you picked your steps along that rough lane. I remember stepping on the grass which was very frosty, just to toughen the soles of my feet for the road ahead.' John even knew the record-holder for barefoot living. He says, 'It was James Rooney who was the clear winner, as he covered the period from St Patrick's Day to Halloween.' When little Molly and Annie walked to school together, they took turns to be on the outside of the path so they would share the burden of greeting other road users who spoke to them.

Life at Breesy is what we would call 'subsistence farming' and they just called 'farming'. Consider, for example, grocery shopping. This was a process which you initiated by bringing some groceries *to* the shop, namely butter and eggs to barter with.

The carefully planned economics behind the system was: 'A dozen of eggs would get me half a pound of tea. Now I need tea, sugar, bacon, barley. How many dozen eggs have I got? Go and see if there is a hen on a nest; if there is, try her. We could wait till she has laid to make up that last dozen. That would cover the cost of most on my list. We must have clean eggs; that one needs a wipe; a wee run of baking soda will take off that stain. Wrap them in newspaper and put them in the basket carefully.'

Now imagine one of the children carrying ten dozen eggs (about five kilos) to the shop. The nearest grocery shop was McGrath's 'over the mountain' – not, in this case, Breesy but Derrynacrannog, a rough heather-clad hill behind their house without a connecting road or lane. When the shopkeeper wrote out the bill and compared the total with the value of the eggs there might be a debit, but the Myles's had always calculated to have the cash ready. 'Run in rags before you run in debt,' was old man Myles's mantra. The barter system also explains why eggs weren't too often on the menu back at home.

Some things had to be bought in Ballyshannon. In jam-making season sugar was bought by the six-kilo bag. The fruit was free – it grew in their own fields. Flour was bought by the 50-kilo sack. Robert Myles, as man of the house, was in charge of this aspect of shopping, using a neighbouring relative's horse and trap. These outings were always 'dress up' occasions. He discarded the everyday cap and out came the hard hat. A special brush, the shape of a broom, only in miniature, was used to make it look respectable.

The children even worked out a way to buy sweets. When one of them was given a penny by somebody (like a friendly relative) they could hand it over at school to Mary McGarrigle whose parents had a shop (miles away). Within twenty-four hours Mary would produce 12 big toffees. Door-to-door delivery!

It would be condescending to think of the Myles children as being unaware of the wider world. They weren't. Every few years their quiet, clever mother took one or another of them on a winter holiday to Glasgow, her original home town. When it came to her turn, Bessie's Glasgow trip was full of wonder. While she and her mother were still on the night ferry from Derry, she discovered the flush toilets. Her memo says, 'I went into one, pulled the chain, enjoyed watching the water gush out, then into another and did likewise and was heading for another when Mum spotted me. "Come back here. You don't keep flushing toilets. The stewardess will scold you." Bessie didn't quite see the logic in that: 'After all, water isn't scarce, the boat is surrounded with it, and there was nobody else in the toilets.'

I can only imagine the wide-eyed amazement of a ten-year-old child going to see the circus for the first time at Kelvin Hall or a Shirley Temple film in the cinema. All the children reported that Glasgow 'smelled different'. What they had detected was coal – something they never used at home (even their school-room was heated by turf supplied in a rota by parents).

Another window into the world was opened by electronics. The Myles family had a cousin, Bob, who had been orphaned at an early age and was being raised by an uncle and aunt, also in the Breesy district. Bob was like having an older brother living up the road. They forgave him for being of little use on the farm or with the cattle because he had a flair for tiny craftsmanship. This extended to building himself a radio, a first for Breesy and the surrounding district. A cable strung across two trees on either side of the road and down into the house served as the antenna. At night that house was busy with people coming to hear the 'talking machine'.

Sunday night was a special case because Bob was able to tune in to the service broadcast by the BBC from St Martin-in-the-Fields church in Trafalgar Square in London. The Myles family, and half the neighbourhood, came over and congregated in the kitchen. The visiting farmers doffed their caps and sat in reverent silence for the duration. Bob was a young man of many parts because, apart from the radio, he already had a significant clientele in South Donegal who needed their watches, clocks or bikes fixed.

He also had a little disciple – Jim, the youngest Myles – who watched and learned this Breesy version of engineering. Jim was much too young to be part of the farm workforce but, after watching Bob's fix-it facility he successfully rigged up a hydroelectric system, generating enough power from the stream at the end of their field to light a bulb in the kitchen. Thus did the people of Breesy get ahead of those in Ballyshannon, who took until the mid-1950s to generate electricity with a hydro station! Did little brother Jim's ingenuity stir in Annie a sneaking regard for electricians?!

It was from my mother's notes that I first learned about Bob building the radio and the Sunday evenings. In fact, my mother surprised me by including, in her Breesy memoirs, matters of the heart – the goings-on between her heart and God. It looks like she had a tender conscience. She could remember being chastised for a fit of temper while still a little girl.

Then, ominously, she remembered, 'When the fever was going round the school I took it later than the others. My throat was so bad the doctor was sent for.' Nobody did that on a whim. It required one of the boys to cycle the seven miles to Ballyshannon as fast as he could to produce Dr Gordon. He came and shone a flashlamp down her throat. She says, 'I don't remember what was prescribed for a cure, but I do remember Dad coming in and praying for me on his knees by the bedside. I never did hear him pray out loud before.' Those were the days before penicillin was available. I can only imagine my grandfather's turmoil as he knelt by Annie's bedside and pled for her life. It moves me to this day.

She recalls an evening when she was ten years old, walking the four miles to a public meeting (after the six-mile round-trip to school!) where someone was going to teach how to personally apply the core teachings of the Bible. This touched her and she wanted to get right

13

with God but was far too shy to ask about the details. It would be another ten years before she got another chance. The Myles home had a Bible with good-sized print and indeed Bertie, John and Bessie made a plan to read through it.

In the meantime a fateful day arrived for the family. Robert Myles was gravely ill. My mother at that stage had left school and was working for a while at the Mall Hosiery factory in Ballyshannon. On her Wednesday half-day off she came home to see her father and, on leaving, said, 'I'll be back to see you on Sunday,' to which he answered, 'The next time I'll see you will be up above.' On Friday he was gone.

One by one the day came for each of them to march off into life – but there was so much life they had already experienced. Bertie and John both went to England – Bertie to work in a factory in Birmingham, John to work on a farm. Molly married Ernie Clarke and ended up in his substantial general store in Ballyshannon. Jim worked in the same store. After working a while in Ballyshannon, Annie found her way to a job in war-time Derry.

But, before Annie left for Derry, Breesy saw another unusual turn of events when two preachers turned up in the district. They pitched (with permission) a big long tent in a potato field and proceeded to expound the Bible every evening for anyone who cared to turn up. One imagines it must have been quite an occasion of comment in the mountain community.

My mother's curiosity got the better of her and she went and listened to a new world of sparkling forgiveness and hope for the future. It sounded to her like a deal not to pass up, so in her own way, she asked God to count her in. Apparently he was delighted to do so because she was never the same thereafter.

Before long the preachers moved on to pastures green (or more likely brown in that part of the world) but not before she marked that auspicious decision to keep following Jesus. Now, the way Christians have done that for over 1900 years is by getting baptised. But what to do in a rural area seven miles outside Ballyshannon? Simple – they baptised her in the nearest body of water, which in this case was a drainage stream. To her dying day my mother regaled anyone who would listen with the story of how she was 'converted in a potato field and baptised in a sheugh'.

I never saw the Breesy house. By the time I was old enough to visit the mountain, the house was gone. It simply fell down, insubstantial in the face of the Donegal elements.

Now Annie was about to face the unfamiliar melting-pot that was Derry in 1943.

CHAPTER 2

THE THIRD-WORST
TOWN

By the time Joe (now an established Derry electrician) married Annie (the manager of the transport café at Guildhall Square) and moved to Strabane, County Tyrone, they had hit on a way to keep their expression of loyalty to Jesus as simple and unpretentious as possible. They took up with fellow-travellers who saw things the same way – the Plymouth Brethren. It seemed the Brethren didn't vote. Apparently they reckoned that their citizenship was in heaven and that's one place they definitely don't vote anyway. Maybe that helped them to navigate a town that takes some getting used to.

Strabane was later introduced to the TV-watching public when an unsuspecting reporter, Charles Witherspoon from Ulster Television, arrived there in 1970 to check on unemployment. A little group of men obligingly protested in front of the Town Hall.

Their self-appointed spokesman was George Cunningham and he had a short statement ready which was captured on camera. It was never clear who captured whom because our George laid into the reporter at the top of his lungs. It sounded like he had served his apprenticeship in an iron-foundry. You can usually find a video clip of George online. So, at 10 out of 10 on the sound dial he gives it the full wellie:

'My wife is employed but I'm not employed and there's a Council inside this Town Hall that doesn't give the…' at which point the valiant Witherspoon says,

'I'm sorry, yir movin round, yi see, an' the camera can't get yi.'

'There's a Council in Strabane' (same volume)

'Wait, wait, wait, take yir time, take yir time…'

'Yiss… We've got a council in Strabane that doesn't give work to the people that's born in the town. They don't give out the houses to the people that's born in the town. I've been threw out several times in the town and I had to go to the minister in Stormont to fight for fair play.'

'Now, just a moment…'

Our man in Strabane had, however, put his finger on the town's main issue, unemployment. Somehow he thought that the Town Hall contained all these jobs that were missing. In the meantime Strabane male unemployment had risen to the highest level of any town in the European Union.

Many years later Channel Four declared Strabane as the third-worst town to live in the United Kingdom. Strabane found that hard to take from a Channel that only made it to number Four – and how closely did Strabane ever enjoy the embrace of the United Kingdom anyway? Channel Four executives were invited to the town to judge for themselves. The next year it was the eighth worst.

Strangely enough, it was to take up employment that my father moved to Strabane in 1946. Joe Wilson, the 29-year old electrician, freshly married to Annie Myles from (seven miles outside of) Ballyshannon, started work with the electricity service, then known as the 'Electricity Board of Northern Ireland'. Despite later name changes this institution was, forever after known to him, to the employees and to our family, simply as 'the Board'. The Board never had a more faithful employee than Joe Wilson.

Strabane gave me my start too. I moved into 18 Church Street in June 1948. All I had known before then was a few days with my mother in Strabane Hospital. House number 18 was just a matter of yards down from 'Dillon's corner', the last bend on the road coming down from Knockavoe mountain, a bend so dangerous that it attracted no accidents since everybody drove round it slowly. By the time my brother (called 'Myles' to preserve the family name) and sister Ruth arrived we had moved a mile uphill. Vehicular traffic seldom made it as far as our house which allowed us that great rural childhood pleasure of guessing who drove by just by recognising the sound of their car's engine. When a strange car ventured this far up the hill the cry would go up, 'Who was that?'

The family almost felt as if we ourselves were working for the Board. Soon our Dad's job entailed being on call every second weekend, ready to respond to emergencies such as power cuts due to extreme weather. Of course, as soon as he left the house it was up to the rest of the family to field all the incoming emergency calls since our telephone number (Strabane 2265) was the only one anybody had.

The number was also just one digit different from the local convent's number. This got us involved unexpectedly in the election of the next pope. After Pope Pius XII died, it seemed like the entire population of Strabane wanted to know if a new pope had been elected. People reckoned that if anyone knew the answer it would be the nuns so they called their number – and often our number too, by mistake. So at home we took it in turns to answer the stray calls, thereby disappointing many. Eventually it struck us to call the convent ourselves and find the right answer. Thereafter, we were able to satisfy callers with the news they wanted, 'John XXIII'!

On one occasion I inadvertently kept the residents of Castlederg without power for an afternoon simply because I couldn't understand the emergency caller who kept saying, 'It's Kane's washer.' Apparently, somebody called Kane had a gravel-washing pit where a JCB had got mixed up with an overhead line. However, 'Kane's washer' was more shorthand than I was trained to decipher.

Those 'call-outs' routinely involved my father driving far into the countryside to switch off the current on the major lines carried by electricity pylons so the system could be worked on. This often meant replacing a fuse.

Now this was not like the fuse in the plug of your bedside table lamp. It was a glass tube about a foot long containing carbon tetrachloride around a spring-loaded coil. And this thing was perched as high as two houses on the pylon overhead. You manhandled the tube into position by attaching it to telescopic fibreglass 'operating rods' which reached up that high. And of course the reason you were there in the first place was that it was blowing gale-force winds. In the middle of the night.

It wasn't always in the middle of the night. Unbelievably, my father would sometimes bring one of us kids with him (usually in day-time). We would watch in a mixture of awe and apprehension as the storm wrestled with the operating rods which weaved around in the sky till, with a quick lunge of our father's strength, they hit their target with a satisfying hiss not unlike a strike of lightning. Maybe that was one of the reasons we thought we all worked for the Board. It certainly provided a unique bonding experience with our Dad and made up for missing him on quite a number of Christmas dinners because he was on call. But a Board employee's Christmas had perks for the family. As kids we always wanted to join my father on his December visit to one of the enterprises to which the Board supplied electricity – Nestlé's chocolate factory. And they did not disappoint us.

Changing fuses also had a side benefit. My father reclaimed the spent fuses – which weren't broken – they just weren't working. So when you took the cap off them you could harvest the carbon tetrachloride which was marvellous as a cleaning agent for textiles. Research later found out that it can affect the central nervous system. Oops! Good job we did most of the cleaning experiments in the back yard.

The Board's territory in Strabane went right up the border on its Western edge and, in the early days, included a technical enclave in Derry, requiring regular visits to the city of his birth. As he drove up Aberfoyle Crescent one day my father remarked, 'I was born twice in that house,' to one of his workmates in the van. There was no response for half a minute and then the man said, 'You what?' 'I was born twice in that house.' 'How come?' 'Being born the first time wasn't enough. I needed to be born again.' Since my father had a stammer, you can imagine the intricacies of that conversation. My father's mischievous explanations of his spiritual life were as unpredictable as they were profound.

Like many of his time, he didn't progress from primary to secondary school but rather to night classes in the city's technical college, known to all as the 'Tech'. This was a rather marvellous education because the primary school gave you a well-rounded education (my father always referred to geometry as 'Euclid') but also allowed you to totally specialise for your apprenticeship. The one thing it couldn't do was lead you to university. And that meant that he was never going to hold the Board's top position in Strabane, that of 'district engineer'. He could only ever rise to 'district foreman' which he proceeded to do.

The lack of a degree never seemed to rankle with him and it also meant that he got to work closely with some amazing district engineers, all of whom learned their key lessons from Joe Wilson, according to himself anyway. But one of these, John Gaston, taught my father a thing or two.

John and my father had more in common than just the Board. The very separate trajectories of their lives had led both of them to decide, in their youth, to follow Jesus. Now these trajectories met in Strabane. So they regarded themselves as brothers. Rather than being a cosy work arrangement it presented its own quandaries. In a town of 9,000 everyone knows your business, especially when it comes to employment. These were the post-war days when ex-servicemen were officially supposed to get preferment so the conduct of Board business was under continual community scrutiny. Steely fairness in hiring and firing and running the Board was the order of the day, led by John and Joe.

One morning my father arrived into work late. Unusual for him. Before long John called him into his office to ask for a reason. My father explained that he had been out late the night before at a gathering of Christian friends, although he was also taken aback somewhat because he knew John had been there too. 'I know,' said

John, 'I was there myself. It's not a reason to be late.' My father readily reported this to us, the family. When I think about it, that took more humility than some fathers have with their children. My guess is that the story somehow leaked around the Board as well. I don't think that's why John Gaston did it. He did it because it was right.

Fair employment practice required the level of vigilance needed to detect chancers. My father caught up with one such employee who, after weeks of absence, was still bringing in scribbled doctor's notes which, upon closer examination, just said 'debility'. My father asked him how his debility was and he said it was much better now. One Board worker lost his job for what my father called 'bad English' – he couldn't tell the difference between 'mine and thine'.

The differences between the Nationalist/Catholic and Unionist/Protestant communities (which were later to produce acrimonious strife) also provided a source of humour for everyone in the 50s and 60s. Leo, who worked for the Board, lived in the district known as 'up the head of the town' with his sister who assured all and sundry, 'I'm not giving my brock to Catholic hens.'

Permit a short digression: 'brock' is kitchen waste which can be made available for feeding poultry and animals, and is collected door-to-door by a brock-man. A folk song about a hapless Derry girl recounts that her intended husband was of such low estate that 'his father was a brock-man from Strabane'. Since we had 'Catholic' and 'Protestant' everything, we had Catholic and Protestant brock-men and consequently Catholic hens (and I suppose by extension there were Protestant hens too).

Strabane seemed to have an endless supply of such 'characters' – like the shabbily dressed man, with suit and tie, who seemed to spend the day chatting to his mates on the street corner with his head tilted to one side listening. He earned the nickname 'the retired violinist'. A man who had previously worked in landscape gardening, laying concrete patio slabs, was referred to by a local newspaper journalist as an 'unemployed slabber' because they had a long-running spat.

Although we spent the first two years of my life at No. 18 Church Street my father then decided that he didn't want his children 'being brought up by every Tom, Dick and Harry on the street' but by himself and my mother. So we moved about that important mile out of the town, to a house rented from my father's uncle, Johnny Kee.

This sounds like the idyllic country life (the address, after all, was 'Greenhurst, Curly Hill') but it had its challenges. We were not connected to the town's sewerage system (thus involving my father in perennial monkeying around with a septic tank), a previous tenant was said to have been murdered there, the building was surrounded by a jungle that would have done the Amazon proud and, most ironic of all, we had no electricity – in 1950 the service just hadn't made it that far out of civilisation.

There were upsides, like the evocative lighting of the oil lamps in the evening with their feathery mantles, the smell of paraffin oil and hiss as the pressure was pumped up. And neither Tom, Dick nor Harry were anywhere to be found. We lived surrounded by cattle, a dairy herd which mostly belonged to the Gormleys who lived three fields away (that's how you counted distance).

Gormleys were rightly proud of two things – they had an up-to-date milking parlour and their herd was 'TB tested'. Tuberculosis was a big deal. My Uncle Jim contracted TB and spent a good part of a year in a sanatorium. These institutions were specially built at the time, housing the patients as far away from each other as possible by positioning the wards in separate buildings around the grounds.

The milk which Gormleys supplied all over town was not pasteurised which was why the herd had to be tested. Nor was it homogenised which was why it tasted like real milk with cream that actually rose to the top. I was fascinated to get a spell of holiday 'work experience' by learning to work the bottle-capping machine.

It was important to stay on the right side of the Gormleys (not difficult to do) because they owned a television and made it available to my brother Myles and me on Saturday afternoons so we could watch *The Lone Ranger*. During our faithful watching of the programme they even served us high-end food and drink – orange squash and Rich Tea biscuits. 'High-end' to boys of that age anyway.

If you came to our house you could tell there were five Wilsons because we were all represented in the garden. Our father had decreed that the surrounding jungle be subdued – and not just subdued but made productive. So the back garden was divided into plots – one for each of us. Dad grew a range of vegetables and our ever-practical and resourceful mother grew potatoes, reckoning that if all else failed, the basics would still be there. She remembered the recent days of rationing and made jam from every kind of berry that dared make a show on a branch – damsons, gooseberries, blackberries – anything free. She once switched from our long-term grocer because he was, in her view, penny-pinching. And when the three of us children were well grown up she returned to work, this time in a hosiery factory in Strabane, Adria Knitting Mills, so the family's finances could continue to support missionaries.

As far as gardening was concerned, my laziness and impatience (I had no time whatsoever for weeding) were expressed in my planting choice – gladioli. I could just stick a few of the big bulbs in my assigned front-row plot in the spring and in the summer – whizz-bang. Visitors to our back garden never said, 'Oh, I do like the potatoes and carrots.' They couldn't see past the gladioli doing their ostentatious thing. I always felt like I was somehow cheating, but I could never figure out to whom I should confess.

For a while the bane of this country life, from our father's point of view, was the flock of jackdaws who took up residence in our chimney every March. Their nests, made from twigs, had a way of rendering our flues all but impassable to the smoke. Not only did the smoke empty out into the living room but, much more dangerous for birds and humans, the twigs caught alight from time to time. As kids we thought this very exciting but our father took a dimmer view because it could set the whole chimney on fire and this could lead to setting the house on fire.

An idea slowly settled on Dad's mind. There was only one thing to be done with the jackdaws. Shoot them. Even if you only hit a couple of them surely that would scare off the rest of the flock. Then into the edge of Dad's mind crept a sub-idea. He knew someone with a shotgun - none other than the son of the Key family, his very own cousin. He was, in effect, our landlord and he surely wouldn't like to hear of the house being burned to the ground by jackdaws. So a discreet visit was paid to the Keys' farmhouse.

That's how a shotgun and ammunition ended up in our hallway. I'm not sure who exactly had the licence for this thing but let's not get technical. Early the next morning, before he went out to work, my father sneaked out to the garden, loaded the shotgun, took note of where the jackdaws were (not difficult – they generated an almighty racket), took aim and bang. It appears that these particular jackdaws weren't stupid. Between our Dad's taking aim and the bang they had transferred from the chimney to a local tree.

He tried again the next morning. Same result. A battle of minds began to unfold, since Dad wasn't stupid either. He was giving them too much time to re-locate. Why not load the gun in the hallway, thus cutting out one stage and being ready the exact moment he emerged out the front door? (A point of detail here – our house had a little raised threshold in the doorstep.)

So the following morning, with somewhat of a swagger, the neophyte gunman loaded the gun, listened for the jackdaws (you could easily hear them from the hallway) and made a run for it. It ended up not so much a run as a step – a step which tripped on that threshold of ours and produced not only a bang but also a hole in the hall ceiling.

I think Joe Wilson was a little late to work that day because, instead of driving his van to the Board's premises, he drove it straight to Keys' and handed over a hot shotgun, scared out of his wits but forever chastened on the subject. The jackdaws held a small champagne reception after Dad had safely gone to work.

Back to that garden over which the jackdaws operated their surveillance: like I said, I wasn't a natural weeder. I thought of my approach as more scientific and effective. One afternoon when my parents were away for the day, they left clear instructions as to how I was to weed the shallots, of which we had a long, raised bed. To me this seemed like work and not suitable for a pleasant Saturday. So I roped in my friend Philip Brown to help – he was our doctor's son who was visiting and surely he would share my technical approach to things. My brainwave was to remove all the plants of every kind from the raised bed – shallots and weeds alike. Then, once the weeds were discarded en masse one could clean off the shallots and pop them back in again. I couldn't imagine how no-one had ever thought of this before.

Apparently there's a good reason why our novel method had remained untried. It doesn't work. It ruins the planting of the shallots. It causes your parents to have to plant new shallots all over again. For me the only good thing that came out of this exercise was Philip's presence. My parents held his father, the doctor, in very high regard so his association with the weeding venture somewhat took the edge of blame off me.

The back garden also accommodated two sheds. One was a hen house. My mother wasn't about to put all that good Donegal hen-keeping training to waste. The other was the 'coal-house'. This had originally been designed to house our coal. In those days the 'coal-man' would come on schedule and manhandle the required number of bags into a bunker within the shed. By the time I was attending secondary school (Strabane Grammar School) I regarded the rest of the coalhouse as my own exclusive scientific laboratory.

Some kind relative had given me a chemistry set at Christmas and that was enough to get me started. I tried every experiment in the instruction booklet and then set off on a teenage scientific career of my own. I started with making cuprammonium crystals – ridiculously easy to make by adding copper sulphate to ammonium. You can easily grow them up to half an inch long and you can easily convince your mother that such a lovely thing makes the whole coalhouse lab a worthwhile pursuit.

Thus emboldened, I went on to make coal-gas using the test-tubes supplied in the set. You could set fire to the little flame of gas. I thought this was appropriate for a coalhouse, never imagining the havoc that would have been wreaked had the whole shed gone up. Manufacture of hydrogen was now calling and I rose to the task. It doesn't burn with a small flame but it explodes with a hopefully small(ish) pop.

Now it was time for pharmaceuticals. It had become known to me that you could write away for mail-order supplies of chemicals if you wanted to mix a new compound (I think it was written on the original cardboard box the set came in). And there was indeed a new compound I wanted to make. Our parents had long extolled the virtues of Andrews Liver Salts and I discovered that it tells you on the tin exactly what's in there (I guess they legally have to). My supplies duly arrived and I did the mix and drank it. I waited and waited but it never produced the normal enema effect. Either I got the formula wrong or I had, by now, developed a cast-iron constitution.

The taste was important – not the taste of the DIY 'Andrews' but the taste of adventure which would soon be applied beyond the chemical world, to the spiritual.

CHAPTER 3

MISSIONARY TENDENCY

If my mother was the original country girl from a windswept mountainside in southern Donegal, my father was the original city boy from Derry. He found it faintly amusing that Belfast people thought they came from a 'city' – which he considered to be a relatively recent start-up. His extended family was a veritable rainbow of religious conviction. He had been born into a Presbyterian family but not far away on the family tree were perched Cooneyites, Exclusives, a spiritually opinionated First World War veteran and a close relative who would promptly and proudly tell you the name of her church, although she didn't actually attend it.

So my parents plumped for simplicity – and who could blame them! Their idea of simplicity had a basic menu which included the Bible, meeting up with like-minded devotees of Jesus, living frugally so they could help those who had fallen on hard times – *and* the backing of missionaries. At the back of my father's mind there may have been a hesitance to go into missionary work himself. He could scarcely speak. As a small child he had woken up one night in shock, and with a stammer, as the last violent vestiges of the War of Independence were being played out on their street. That stammer stayed with him the rest of his life and although we as children found it excruciating to watch him converse with visitors, it never prevented him from living a full and cheerful life.

It so happened that Strabane had already produced two missionaries to Japan, which are normally as scarce as hen's teeth. It was therefore inevitable that we would somehow get mixed up with them – Eva Glass and Bobbie Wright, and then others. They succeeded in making Japan, which seemed so impossibly far away, a reality to the sturdy, phlegmatic residents of Strabane.

For example, on my desk, to this day, I have a little wooden Japanese doll (called a *kokeshi*). It was sent to us by Eva Glass from Hokkaido in northern Japan in the early 1950s. A *kokeshi* has no arms or legs but has a head that squeaks as it's moved around. The family was delighted with this highly ornamented 11-centimetre-long creation. In later correspondence with Eva we found out that you can screw off the base of the *kokeshi* to reveal an inner compartment in which a message can be hidden. And so it was in the slightly later 1950s that we discovered the greeting that Eva had originally sent!

At one point it struck my parents that it would be a nice touch to send a Christmas care package to these Irish people they knew in Japan – which now included at least three families. So every year in mid-November they would assemble generous packages of chocolate, no less, to be shipped off in good time.

Now, it concentrates the mind of a small child to see chocolate *leaving* his house in such quantities at that time of year. I should have known – on the wall of our sitting room there was a plaque which displayed for all to see my parents' philosophy of life. It said, 'Seek ye first the kingdom of God, and his righteousness; and all these things shall be added unto you. Matthew 6:33.' It was burned into the wood with an iron poker.

Bobbie Wright, a son of the town, had already gone to Japan in the 1930s, ostensibly to be a pharmacist (and he was a good one) but actually to progress the Christian gospel. His idea was to demonstrate by his practice of business that his highest allegiance was to Christ.

Eventually, during the Second World War, the Japanese authorities tumbled to this and interned him because he wouldn't switch that highest allegiance to Emperor Hirohito. He had taken up the offer of a sailing to Canada but halfway there the ship did a U-turn and sailed back to Yokohama. Pearl Harbour had intervened. His cellmate, another missionary called John Hewitt, died in the prison. By the time Bobbie was released he weighed just over 50 kilos and his hair had turned white.

Amazingly, all Bobbie wanted to do after the war was return to a devastated Tokyo with his wife Eirene and family and set up home in the ruins. And he wanted to go to prison – but this time to help prisoners in whatever way he and his wife could. He was invited to provide recreation and education – which led to being given permission to run Bible studies for all kinds of inmates. Some were psychotic, violent men, some murderers, some black-marketeers, both Japanese and US servicemen.

Bobbie had successfully lobbied to ensure that prison welfare was enshrined in Japanese law, and when he eventually was forced to leave Japan to seek treatment for an inoperable back injury, he was presented with an illuminated statement of congratulation and a silver memorial cup by the new Minister of Justice at an elaborate ceremony. He was also given the opportunity to broadcast to all the prisoners in Japan for ten minutes over closed-circuit TV. He was then stretchered on to the ship for the voyage back to Ireland.

When the Wrights appeared back in Strabane on a year-long visit they moved into a house in Church Street only to find that they couldn't easily fit all their six children into the house. So the extra child (Annesley) was offered to live with us, 'up the hill', for that year. He didn't seem at all bothered to be the left-over child and so our family had an extra brother for a year – and after all, the rest of his family was scarcely a mile away. By my early teens it seemed logical to me that I was learning Japanese with Linguaphone records.

The time had come for me to transfer to the local secondary school, Strabane Grammar School, which had been opened two years before to great fanfare.

I went with my father to be interviewed by the shiny new principal, James Wilson (no relation). He was a staunchly self-professed atheist so he was somewhat taken aback when he asked me, 'What do you want to do when you grow up?' and I replied, 'I want to be a missionary.' He adjusted his rimless glasses and said two words to my father: 'Passing fancy?' to which my heroic father replied (you'll just have to imagine the stammer), 'No, that's really what he wants to do.'

My father was holding this conversation in an imaginary world since neither he nor my mother had experienced anything 'secondary' about education. Now he was entering me into a lighthouse educational institution that introduced me to George Orwell through 'Politics and the English language', Seán O'Casey through 'The Plough and the Stars', and that same James Wilson who instilled in me his excellent vision of practising Physics with clinical precision. Amongst the subjects taught, the odd one out was 'Religion'. It was not entered for State exams so nobody cared too much. Nobody, that is, apart from the Rev Milligan from the nearby village of Ardstraw who was drafted in to teach the Old Testament book of Amos.

I was fascinated. Here was a man who knew his Hebrew language and could make this ancient prophet positively sing. I gobbled it up. The class was like a conversation between Mr Milligan and me. Like I said, nobody else cared. I won the Walter Elliott Religion Education prize. You might think that would warm my parents' hearts. But not quite. Walter Elliott was a local solicitor whose idea of ecumenism was not simplicity (like my parents) but backing all the horses in the denominational race. He tried to believe everything. And as for my parents' view of the Rev Milligan – OK he had good Hebrew, but he was a smoker! Surely Ardstraw could do better than that!

Indeed, Ardstraw had already distinguished itself in our eyes because we treasured one of its own, Eva Warke, who had gone as a missionary nurse to Angola. When missionaries were forced to leave, she simply moved over to Zambia with her steadfast team mate, Emily Rowntree. From there they wrote letters to their friend George Hall in Belfast with reports like:

'We distributed prizes in two Sunday Schools last week and were very pleased with the number of students who had memorised Bible chapters. One girl had memorised 26 chapters and a boy had memorised 25.

'Recently, we experienced the hand of God in a special way. We had spent the weekend at Chavuma and, when we returned here, heard that two armed robbers had been captured. They arrived shortly after we left and were waiting for our return. Some of the local people reported them to the authorities and soldiers found them lying asleep a short distance from our house. They had an AK47 rifle, which was fully loaded; no doubt they were set on getting money and taking the Land Rover.'[1] Seven years later they wrote to George again: 'We have

---

1   Harvest Fields, May-June, 1997

been busy distributing Sunday School prizes. One boy repeated all the Gospel by Mark and part of the Epistle to the Romans.'[2] Eventually, Queen Elizabeth gave Emily an MBE.

How any of this was going to prepare me for missionary work was a question never far from my mind. I had read the old tomes of biographies that told the tales of missionary doctors like David Livingstone. Maybe I should be a doctor and get serious about the biological sciences (after all I had attempted to breed newts, found in a nearby quarry, in a makeshift aquarium under my bed). But it was not to be. My parents' instinctive intuition woke up and advised me that being a doctor was too much for me to aim for.

Meanwhile there was a simple realisation hurtling towards me – how authentic would any kind of fancy mission work be if it didn't work right there in Strabane, let alone on the far side of the world? But how would one address oneself to Strabane collectively? The solution was hiding in plain sight. There was one occasion per year when Strabane gathered itself together, despite any tribal differences – the Carricklee Races.

This was a point-to-point event held every St. Patrick's Day just outside the town. You could have a nice cup of tea in the marquee, maybe a wee drink and, let's not forget, a flutter on the horses from stables all over Ireland. The chairman of the event was one Dan Smyth. Dan occupied three positions in our firmament.

2   Harvest Fields, March-April 2000

He was the owner of Smyth's Mills in Strabane producing animal feed (a treasured commodity) *and* he was the chair of the Carricklee Races *and* he was a director of the Electricity Board for Northern Ireland – that very Board who employed my father (and the rest of the family, as we saw it).

I was advised that only Dan Smyth could give the go-ahead for my scheme to occupy one of the stands at the races for the sale of high-quality, low-price copies of the Gospels. On the appointed day I went to his office in the mill to hear the verdict. It wasn't the verdict I was looking for. He thought he knew more about racing than I did – and he wasn't wrong! 'It's not exactly a Bible-reading moment,' was his final word and despite my positive assurance that any moment could be a Bible-reading moment, he wouldn't budge.

My gallant father, who had fully supported my approach to his boss's boss's boss, then also complied with Plan B. The key to this plan was that he knew every lane in the Strabane district, including the one that led to the Racecourse entrance. I had a (fresh new) driving licence so he drove me to Derry, we hired a small van, I drove it back, stocked it with the aforementioned Gospels and parked it on the grass verge beside that entrance lane. The public had a great day at the races that 17th March because they had unfettered access to great reading material on the way in and out, without the clutter of other stands.

The next event on my horizon was to leave home, leave Strabane and go to college. It seemed the decent thing to do, before I would go, to meet our townful of neighbours on a more individual basis – better than the shallow kind of chat you might get with the crushing crowds on a race day. Again, the Board came to my assistance. Because they supplied electricity to everyone in town they needed to know where every single house was. So they made use of a very large ordnance survey map, which was replaced every few years – I guess to accommodate the possibility of new places being built. They threw the old ones away which is how they came into my possession (although they might as well have kept them since the likelihood of anybody building new houses in Strabane was pretty remote!).

The map allowed me not to miss anybody over the next few months. I found there was no correlation whatsoever between what people really believed and their social status, denomination or politics. When I arrived at somebody's front door unannounced with Bible materials (and of course the Board's map) on the carrier of my bike there was simply no telling what they would say.

Funnily enough, nobody suspected me of being a Jehovah's Witness or a Mormon – I just didn't fit that image. One guy seemed vastly relieved that he could now talk to somebody about the Bible which he had read privately at home for years. One woman told me where to get lost because she thought I was soft in the head.

Overall, the experience was an eye-opener, or maybe best said, an ear-opener. There was no such thing as the general public. Everyone had their own sense of where the dial stood as they measured their relationship with God. Some were stuck, some unsure, some open to try a Bible view on the subject. But many were open to chat. I didn't run into many atheists.

Some Donegal people regarded Strabane (and not Lifford) as if it were their county town. The border was so thin you could hardly see it. It struck me that people in the surrounding Donegal towns would be as open to talk as the locals were. By the time I left home I had acquired a working familiarity with the hinterland of Lifford. Same bike, same Bible, no need for a map (it's hard to miss Donegal). But since everything was further away it required a weather forecast.

A few months later I had a sudden wake-up call one day to the fact that not everybody was as open to chat. I had just left Strabane (and Donegal, the Board, the lot) behind me forever to study in Trinity College Dublin, courtesy of County Tyrone who paid all my fees and maintenance, since the means test showed my parents to be less than financially flush. Trinity processed you in your first week, getting you fixed up with a library card, a schedule of lectures, lab hours (I was going to study microbiology) *and* an appointment with your tutor who would sign your form as being *in loco parentis* – in the place of parents (couldn't help thinking, 'Good luck with that!').

Nobody had told me about this 'tutoring' thing. All I knew was what you see in popular culture about Oxford and Cambridge where a ring of dutiful, doting students arrange themselves around an avuncular professor who dispenses knowledge to them in mercifully bite-sized chunks. I was curious to know how they would do this with microbiology. I headed to what they call the 'back' of College to meet my tutor in his office (curiously in the Physics department).

He signed the form as per normal and then asked me what I'd like to do after I graduated. By now you know that I said, 'I want to be a missionary.' That didn't suit him at all. 'I hope you don't start that kind of thing around here!' he replied. 'Well, actually, I hope to do just that. Indeed, I have a Bible here in my pocket for when I need it.' I had just lit the touch-paper on his explosive rocket. The next five minutes was a rant against Christian faith, missionaries and the Bible, to which he took great exception. 'If that were to be published today it would be banned as obscene!' he now roared. The onslaught was so total that all I could murmur was, 'I believe the Bible from beginning to end so I'm going to have to take my business elsewhere,' and I walked out, although I had no idea of where I would 'take my business'.

Now I had a new question – had I scuppered my chances of a college education because I couldn't have a civilised conversation with my tutor? I asked around and found that my tutor would have little to do with my college career, the appointment was merely a perfunctory obligation and I already had from him all I needed – the signed form. I never saw him again in my life.

Little did he know it, but the tutor's intervention put iron in my backbone. I would treat the citizens of Dublin just as I had learned in Strabane and Donegal. Before long I had an arrangement to share time on a city-centre book-barrow that offered a good range of portions of the New Testament. Of course, to trade like that on the street you needed a certificate (now called a 'casual trading licence'). Which makes sense of what I wrote in my diary for later that year: I had 'almost forgotten to renew my pedlar's certificate'. Horrors!

Every one of us in our house had a missionary tendency – and the source of that reflex reaction points to the Plymouth Brethren.

CHAPTER 4

THE MEETING

The 'Brethren' was (and is) a gloriously modest movement of Jesus-followers whose simple approach emanated, not from Plymouth, but from North Wicklow of all places. This simplicity principle seems to have worked, since they have poured out an astonishing stream of linguists, public servants, writers, university academics, missionaries, poets and scientists.

The Wilsons didn't join – nobody 'joined'; there was no joining to do. They were never interested in some sort of denominational 'signing up'. Their guideline was, 'Any friend of Jesus is a friend of ours.'

I'm not sure that Joe and Annie were unnecessarily worried about Plymouth or Wicklow. They just wanted to meet and work for God with a few like-minded friends. The friends in Strabane didn't look at all like poets or scientists – more like tradesmen, farmers and shopkeepers. They referred to themselves as 'the Assembly' which sounds rather grand and was better captured by the everyday word we so often used, the 'Meeting'.

And boy, did we meet. On Tuesday evenings we met to study the Bible (obviously), on Friday evening to pray, on Sunday morning for a super-simple version of Communion, Sunday afternoon for Sunday School (which was indeed like school) and, wait for it, Sunday evening again for someone to expand on a Bible passage with personal application. So what would we do on Mondays, Wednesdays and Saturdays? Fear not, we had the occasional meeting for international visitors to deliver a report, because this small (you'd have to say miniscule) group supported missionary work all over the world.

It was not at all unusual, although it was exciting, to hear from a visiting missionary about the latest situation in Venezuela, Congo, Malaysia, Tibet or wherever. Just by sitting there for a couple of years, any child would get at least a medium-level course in human geography. This is as good as you'd get in a lot of secondary education.

You got history too. Simply by reading the Bible a child would encounter the civilisations of the ancient Egyptians, the Persians, the Greeks, the Roman empire and the first millennium of the Jewish people. Tranquil Strabane wasn't a bad place to get this kind of cultural grounding. And kids without any additional schooling would (and do) get those same basics if they are in a similar upbringing in Congo, India – or New York for that matter.

What the Meeting lacked in quantity it made up for in personality. You had the McMonigle family from a farm halfway to Derry, where the ancient Mr McMonigle senior made short shrift of the argument of a couple of young Jehovah's Witnesses who made it as far as his farm door. They claimed that Jesus had reappeared years ago. But they were too young. 'Do you people believe that the church of God went home to heaven in 1917?' asked the farming pensioner. 'Yes we do – exactly.' 'Well I joined the church of God in 1913 and I thinka woulda heerd aboot it.'

His home-spun theology was nothing like as thorough as Lottie McCreedy's, whom I remember fondly as my Sunday School teacher. She started me on memorising Bible passages – just a little at first, then longer ones – like a whole chapter. When I was about ten I was asked, in all seriousness, which *book* of the Bible I would now like to learn. And I said, also in all seriousness, 'The letter to the Hebrews'. That used up the next year or so, but I got there in the end. It's funny how, still to this day, the ancient wisdom in that book comes back to jog my memory and caution my steps.

Or take the case of Harry Wilson (no relation – we Wilsons are as cheap as chips!). Harry was a figure of fun to some of the customers in the draper's shop where he worked because he was 'always going on about the Bible'. Harry hadn't had a cross-cultural communications course in how to deal with regular human beings. He had no fancy education at all. They called him 'The man of one Book'. But, lo and behold, he decides one day that God has guided him to become a missionary to Brazil.

The wise ones of the Meeting mulled that over for a while, a good while, and eventually let him go, wondering, just a little bit, whatever would happen to our Harry. Contrary to expectations, Harry landed in Brazil, learned Portuguese, and launched into years of giving successful Bible courses all over the place. Before long we were hearing of his grateful listeners from the most tropical-sounding locations like Rio Grande Do Sul and Porto Alegre.

I mention 'wise ones' because the Meeting was run by a small group of local lay people. Nobody was ordained. Nobody felt the need. When we met on Sunday morning it was a quiet affair. Whoever had something to say, said it – usually a thought about a Bible passage. Or maybe somebody would pray for a bit. We did a lot of reflecting – by which I mean sitting in silence. Silence was OK with us. All this was interspersed with hymns which we sang, unaccompanied, from the only printed document ever used by the Meeting (apart from the Bible) – 'The Believer's Hymnbook'.

Sunday morning singing could spring its own surprises. On one famous occasion a hymn drew to a close and everybody slowly sat down again. Except my father, who was in his own reverie and oblivious to his now seated comrades. Apparently he remembered a verse that the others didn't, namely 'O that with yonder sacred throng…' As he was realising that he was the last man standing, he had already bellowed out just the 'O'.

The singing especially suited my father. He liked

singing and, like many stammerers who sing well but don't speak fluently, it offered a welcome outlet of emotion and thought. So music had a hallowed place in our house. He sang in choirs. We all charged off to hear him sing in the Male Voice Festival in Derry. We were surrounded by music too at the Derry *feis* to which I was gently dragged (I was scarcely a toddler!) to recite poetry. After having our baths on Saturday nights we sat around and listened to Céilí House from Radio Éireann, or as my father always called it 'Athlone' since that was where the Midlands transmitter was. The tinny signal manfully struggled its way up through the seven counties to reach the Wilsons' big wooden radio beside the fire in the sitting room.

The 'Meeting' occupied the Gospel Hall in the Railway Road. Back in the day it was quite a thing to be near the railway. We had a railway before Belfast and operated the largest rail junction in Ireland during the first half of the 20th century. We had trains (proper steam trains) that ran to glamorous destinations like Ballyshannon. The Belfast train transported the mail and sported a post-box in the side of the mail carriage through which a letter could be posted at literally the last moment if you ran down the Railway Road.

I hasten to say that the Gospel Hall wasn't a church (they would have 'conniptions' at the thought). Why did these 'halls' appear across the rural North in the 1920s, at around 20 miles distant from each other? Simple. The early preachers travelled by bicycle and that was their average day's journey as they moved their things from one district to another.

A 'hall', often a little corrugated iron building, was a preaching station from which they could offer the story of the gospel to all-comers. Since things were going to stay simple, the building never developed beyond being a 'hall' for the 'gospel'. Our hall never developed very far. Bare wooden floor. Bare wooden benches (our posteriors certainly developed). Bare walls. Oh yes – and one refinement - a tank set into the wooden floor in which to baptise anybody who asked for this sign of identification with Christ. Baptism still didn't join you to a denomination which was, by definition, unjoinable.

I asked and they organised it for me. I remember the day. They removed the covering in the floor to reveal the tank which had an immersion heater dangling cleverly in it. I still wonder if some key person forgot to switch on the heater because, when I got in, it still felt like the fourteenth of November. The plan was for me to be baptised by our friend Leonard Mullan, a visiting missionary from, would you believe, Japan.

He thought it would be a good idea to give a little explanation first (remember I was already in the water!). He explained that the significance of the event was my relation to Christ and not to him as a well-known person and so he had asked a local gentlemen in the Meeting to actually do the baptising. He also thought it would be a good idea to sing a hymn first. I had never sung a hymn before, standing in cold water up to my tummy. I knew the hymn. It's quite a long one. The local gentleman got me through the process with no hypothermia. After all that anonymity, he deserves that you know his name! – Hubert Neely.

Leonard Mullan's interest in my case didn't wane. He wasn't long back in Japan when he and his wife Agnes wrote me a chatty letter exactly describing their spare bedroom which they would make available to me if I were ever in the area and asking, 'How is your Japanese coming along?' Apparently that room was 'three mats' (five square metres) in size but, despite their sincere and kind offer, I haven't yet been in the area, or the country for that matter.

Some of the Meeting's activities simply didn't fit in the Hall. At one point we reconvened in Albert Wright's shop in the evenings for a special project. Albert, a highly respected businessman (and secret philanthropist), ran a department store in the centre of town, just up the street from the 'Board'. It served a large catchment area, including the farmers who came to the weekly cattle mart and their wives who had higher fashion on their minds.

On this occasion Albert rearranged the large spaces on the shop's counters to allow us to pack letters. The Meeting had decided to post a letter to every house in one Irish county (we chose Galway) to offer a free sample of Biblical selections. I can't imagine that any direct mail-house would have been more efficient. Not many of them would have hand-written the addresses to an entire county. It appears to me that Albert must surely have helped to finance the project too. Typical of his open-handedness. Years after his early death I discovered that he was also financing the education of a poor family in town who just wouldn't have managed otherwise.

The Meeting grew – occasionally. One of those occasions began when my parents received a letter from a Belfast couple whom they scarcely knew. The letter said that their son, Ronnie, was going to work in Strabane in the Post Office and they were afraid for him because he was running away from God (Ronnie later confirmed this – he thought that Strabane would be a perfect place to run to!). My parents tracked him down (not hard – he did work in the Post Office after all!) and invited him to dinner. They had a cordial chat, nothing special, although my Dad, stammer and all, mentioned that they were committed Christians. After Ronnie had said goodnight he vowed never to see the Wilsons again and got stuck into selling stamps to the Strabane population.

But Ronnie did come back to see the Wilsons – after four years. He said that the trouble with selling the stamps was that he could see out of the high window of the Post Office. He told my father, 'I could see the top of your Electricity Board van every time you went to work and every time you came home. And lunchtime both ways again. All I could see was the big capital "E" which was the first letter of "Eternity" '.

It scared the living daylights out of him. After four years of my father's unwitting effect of driving home for lunch, Ronnie turned himself in – to God, that is, not to my parents. Somewhat to his astonishment he found that God was waiting for him, forgave him (sure why wouldn't he, if Jesus had paid for him) and started him off on a completely new direction in life. The effect, almost instantaneous, was soon visible in his face. And on a surprise return visit to our home, my father was as amazed as anybody else at Ronnie's story.

We held an annual conference every June. After all, where would a Meeting be without a conference! This time there were great numbers of participants, perspiring speakers from around the country and the world, tight parking of cars, country kettles full of tea ('with or without sugar, madam?') and trays full of ham sandwiches, always with mustard – no 'with or without' about that. Since it was June it was often hot, so all the windows were open to prevent the Bible teaching having an unintended soporific effect.

We were treated to the best scholarship the Meeting could attract. It came from sometimes unlikely sources - like Scottish Davy Craig. Davy went to work in the mines (yes, in Scotland) at the age of 16 and studied the Bible at night, after a 12-hour shift, by lamplight. Maybe an unusual activity for a teenager but it produced a scholar whose humility matched his knowledge of Greek by the time he came to us decades later.

When we were kids all this paled into insignificance compared to the Sunday School Outing to Portrush. We decanted out of the hired bus, avoided the welcoming beach, and marched straight into the den of iniquity which was Barry's Amusement Arcade (depends which way you look at it). Which may explain the odd photo in our family album, inscribed on the back as the annual 'Sunday School outing'. It shows no children, despite there only being children in the Sunday School. It shows no women, despite the fact that the lion's share of the teaching work was done by women. What it does show is a group of four more-than-middle-aged men from the Meeting, in suits (of course), standing on the beach. Two of them are wearing hats. They are Nixon Huey (hat), Bobby Sproule, Sam Gourley (hat) and Bill Thompson (should have thought of a hat).

Although they are all distinctive looking, Sam takes the biscuit. His pork-pie hat crowns a head that is also graced with sunglasses (it certainly wasn't sunshine – something to do with his eyes, I think). He is looking straight at you (or so it appears). His left hand is in his pocket, the other behind his back. Try that yourself in the mirror, head erect, chest out, jacket open, tie (if you're wearing one) flapping sideways in the breeze, and see what you look like. You will see a person at ease with himself.

One element of unease does creep into the picture of Sam Gourley, mind you. His braces are so well tightened that they are grabbing his trousers up to an all-time high, giving you a shadow of concern for any next generation of Gourleys. Highly polished leather shoes finish off Sam's beach ensemble.

Nixon also stands erect, both hands in his pockets.

He looks off into the distance, obviously the group's philosopher. He only manages a flat cap although it is obviously his Sunday-go-to-meeting cap, not one you would wear around the farmyard.

Bobby Sproule's head is somewhat bowed, as if in prayer. There is a certain untidiness to Bobby (compared to the others). His thumb is stuck into the waistband of his trousers and his shoes are unpolished.

No matter what way I look at the photograph it looks like Bill Thompson (who is facing the camera side-on) is not wearing a tie. Unbelievable I know, but there you are. He is sporting two pens in his jacket pocket (after all he was the manager of the mill in Raphoe, County Donegal). Bill inclines slightly forward and you know he is murmuring under his breath, 'Men, someone is taking a snap.'

The Meeting had the odd crisis – like when a guy appeared from what one would now call 'another jurisdiction' and joined us. He turned out to be a paedophile and the police caught up with him before we knew what was happening and before he damaged any local children. But the meeting was mostly Bible, prayer, changing the world. Some members were prone to falling asleep when we met. Some called us boring. I can see why. I can even remember the boringness!

But I owe my earliest memory to my father, long before I was familiar with the Gospel Hall. I remember distinctly lying in bed listening to my father's voice. He was singing to me the song 'When Mothers of Salem their children brought to Jesus', which tells the story of Jesus accepting little children despite the objections of the disciples who thought he would surely be above that kind of thing. If I sit still, even now, my memory can exactly reproduce his voice singing it again.

Once I was going to school it was my father again who stammered through an explanation so I could understand how to submit my stubborn little will to Christ. I did. It took me all evening. It took him the first half of the evening to explain.

Although my parents were fans of simplicity, they were never going to imply that we were the only Christians in town, something they also expressed in the Meeting from time to time. Strabane would have been claustrophobic for anyone that narrow-minded. Anyway, we soon found a new escape valve for all that extra pent-up zeal.

CHAPTER 5

GOSPEL LITERATURE DISTRIBUTION

The late-night activity in 1963 to send Bible literature mailshots from the counter of Albert Wright's shop didn't originate in Strabane – and it was only the beginning. The self-effacing genius who had invented that idea turned up one day in the town to promote his next brainwave. It was a brainwave for the summer, which suited me just fine. Teams of us, from around the country, would gather in locations along the western seaboard, almost exactly along the 'Wild Atlantic Way' of later years. We would live frugally (most of us didn't know any other way) and we would simply visit every house in each county.

The genius, a Trinity graduate student called Arthur Williamson, spearheaded the operation himself. Happily, he had a friend called Bert Gray, who was a dab hand at caravans, so I spent a good bit of the summers in the mid-1960s close to nature, as she expresses herself in Mayo and Galway. We couldn't help but get educated. I looked out of the caravan window in Newport, County Mayo one morning to see a ship at the dock beside us loading seaweed en route to the Netherlands. I hadn't known that ships could dock there, nor what on earth Dutch people would be doing with our seaweed, nor how (as it was patiently explained to me) the Dutch were going to turn this into lipstick. I hadn't even heard of Newport before – I had thought that Westport was all the ports you were going to see in Mayo.

Arthur was from Armagh and he had a penchant for new ideas. He would float every new wheeze with the words, 'Some of us were thinking that…'. I asked him later if there was anyone with whom he was in cahoots and he cheerily replied, 'I was mostly in cahoots with myself!' That explained a lot of things.

It wasn't hard to get to work in the morning – we walked. We were only going up the road to whatever house was next on our large-scale map of the county. On the whole people were exceptionally generous with their time, their tea and their innermost thoughts. After all, we were just door-to-door salesmen of Bible portions. But there's nothing like the company of people who will discuss the big issues of life together – those issues that remain unmentionable so much of the time because there's no-one who'll talk about them without embarrassment.

We must have been physically fit with all that walking but we were a dietician's nightmare. Lunchtime would see us sitting on a Mayo hill-top, watching rainclouds scudding by, while we ate white-bread sandwiches containing the day's random rations, like a mixture of cheese and jam. Genius Arthur assured us that this combination would be good for us because 'they eat it in America'.

We never made a profit – maybe because we spent the time and energy on the fireside chats – but we sold good stuff. Most popular was *The Gospels*, translated by Monsignor Ronald Knox, closely followed in popularity by his translation of *The Letters of St Paul*. Each of these books could be had for the price of a packet of cigarettes. There was a reason for all these sales. It wasn't that this translation of the Gospels was all the rage. In fact, you would never run into them in any normal day's work and the nearest bookshop was half a county away.

The Vatican was just starting to grind through a couple of years of their 'Second Vatican Council' when they suddenly released the Bible to the masses. Except the masses in the rural West of Ireland couldn't easily get their hands on a 'released' copy. Then, hey presto, we turned up. A woman in Clare told us she found her younger son reading a copy of the Gospels in bed at midnight. He got it from his older brother and *he* bought it the previous day in a local pub - the kind of distribution Amazon can only dream of!

There was another curious best-seller, *Peace With God* by the American evangelist Billy Graham. Why was he so popular in deepest Connemara? Because Graham's weekly radio programme *The Hour of Decision*, broadcast from Radio Monte Carlo, was 'must listening' in various households. Some volunteered to show us that they even knew Graham's mailing address, 'BGEA, Minneapolis, Minnesota'. Of course, Connemara was nearer to the US in the 1960s than it is today. So many émigrés were sending money back to the valley they came from that I saw some shops that still accepted dollars cash in payment.

Some of us returned to these valleys with yet another popular product – wall calendars. But not any old calendars. These ones had an attractive design for each month along with a suitable verse from the Bible. Our calendar visits were popular because they were in December – we didn't just operate in the balmy Irish summer! The first December operation saw us in Strandhill, County Sligo, where one of our customers, an ex-ship's captain, was happy to tell us he had actually met Billy Graham!

It still puzzles us pleasantly that those we visited were so forthcoming in opening their thoughts and unburdening their hearts. Maybe people just feel more free to respond to un-connected outsiders, but I wonder. I remember well talking to a woman on her doorstep in Oughterard. I explained my reason for being there and showed her our most popular wares – the Gospels and the Letters of Paul. Her interest seemed lukewarm and I was ready to take my leave politely when she told me she couldn't think clearly because a family member was in all kinds of medical trouble. As it happened, I had with me that day a booklet with selections from the Psalms and I read to her from Psalm 34: 'The Lord is near to the broken-hearted, and saves the crushed in spirit.' She cried with gratitude that God had somehow connected with her. Later it struck me – here was a grown woman crying with me at her front door and I was scarcely nineteen years old.

We also got an up-close-and-personal insight into Gaeltacht life, which was a new planet to me. I wandered in with a flimsy, rose-coloured view of the language as a marker of Irish identity, with nothing but Synge's *The Playboy of the Western World* to guide me. Soon I found how nuanced that subject was – like the man who explained to me why he was angry that the Government had not provided enough learning of *English*. He, and so many others, had taken the route to work called the Dún Laoghaire-Holyhead ferry and found himself on a London building site not able to understand what he was being told.

A bright spark amongst us (it could have been the self-effacing genius) came up with a great question – 'What would happen if, instead of marching round the country introducing the Bible, we set up a professional exhibition about the Bible to see if discerning members of the public would *come to us* if we put some effort into publicising it?' It was the right question. Teachers in particular were looking for good material for use in secondary schools.

Our 'Bible Exhibition' was all you ever wanted to know about the Bible but didn't know the questions.

The Exhibition enjoyed a great outing at a teachers' event in Dublin which was under the patronage of the fabled Brian Lenihan, then Minister of Education. I made jolly sure the exhibition came to Strabane and to my delighted consternation 200 people turned up. It did the rounds – Castlebar, Sligo town, Ballina and Athlone. We installed it in a big hotel in Eyre Square in Galway – about 100 nuns came to see that one. But we never actually gave up going to visit people in their homes. When the exhibition came to Galway we took the opportunity to visit every home in the city. Twice.

The photos show that the exhibition was much enhanced by having a glamorous-looking member of our team on hand to inspire the nuns, the curious and the all-comers. Her name was Pam Serdahl and she had burst on my consciousness the previous summer in County Sligo. All I remember is that we were in a schoolhouse in a field in Sligo (why a school in a field I don't know).

This was a welcome change of pace at a weekly get-together by the guys and girls (who worked on different teams during the week). I was giving a talk to the assembled company and one of them (a girl in the front row) laughed at my jokes. At least that's what I thought she was doing because the wide and floppy Parisian-style hat she was wearing underwent convulsions which I took as a good sign. But she was obviously out of my league. I wasn't even sure if I was in a league. Little did I guess that she would become my wife. Eventually. I could not have imagined that a new branch of the family tree was soon to graft me on to it.

Pam, who had moved from northern California, divided her time between the summer field work and secretarial responsibilities organising the whole thing the rest of the year, from an office in Fenian Street in Dublin which has now been subsumed into the Davenport Hotel. Of more recent times Pam and I talked to a manager at the Davenport and suggested there be a re-union in the hotel of all those of us connected with '34A Fenian Street' but he'd never heard of our history and thought it was a bit far-fetched. I think he missed a good opportunity!

Meanwhile, not a million miles from Fenian Street (how convenient!) I was pursuing a degree in microbiology in Trinity College Dublin. I had to remind myself that this meant taking 'time out' in the winter season to go to lectures, do lab work and read books about creatures so small you can't see them. In the midst of my last college year a few Dublin worthies acquired a premises in D'Olier Street that was to serve as a permanent Bible bookshop, still within the geographical orbit of Pam Serdahl.

The building belonged to the *Irish Times* which in those days was next door to the shop. A competent bookshop manager was recruited but there was a slight gap in the schedule before she got there. So somebody with little grasp of my *in*competence imagined I could manage it for a while. In a lapse of judgement, and against the advice of friends, academic and otherwise, I did it. We didn't make any money during that time.

We did stay open – so that's something. The main thing I remember is window-dressing.

When I arrived the shop window was cluttered with little booklets about the Bible, which I thought looked like litter. I also thought it made us look like purveyors of 'little-booklet religion'. I cleared it all out and positioned in the window the biggest possible books I could find in the shop. Into each of them I inserted a flame-shaped paper about one metre tall and coloured neon orange and red. You were supposed to get the idea that proper books are good and world-changing. I'm not sure what the Dublin population made of it but one of the 'worthies' thought it looked unnecessarily revolutionary. Within a five-minute walk there were already two revolutionary bookshops – one for Chinese communism and one for the Russian variety.

It happened that Pam Serdahl was a bit of a spiritual revolutionary herself. By this time she was living in Clarinda Park in Dun Laoghaire and opening her flat at the weekend to a growing circle of South County Dublin friends who felt iffy about the Church, agnostic about God, but were quite keen on Jesus. This miscellaneous crew would spend the evening going over the actual words of Jesus (using the Gospel of Mark). One of them, a Dún Laoghaire postman, was a keen Marxist and a playwright. Another, Martin, was conspicuous because he always looked cold and because he wore an Army Reserve coat – then known as an 'FCA' coat after the Irish acronym for the Army Reserve 'Fórsa Cosanta Áitiúil'.

Mind you, many a guy who wore a 'borrowed' FCA coat was far from being in the Army! Martin was regularly accompanied by Willie from whom he procured his drug supply. Never really qualifying as a drug 'baron', Willie just considered himself as 'helpful'.

Altogether there must have been about a dozen of us, Pam served a bowl of soup about six o'clock in the evening and then we got down to Mark's Gospel. Sometimes it was midnight before the last straggler left. The group gloried under the name of the 'New Ireland Arts Laboratory' (NIAL). I guess that was because (a) we were doing free-thinking research on how to live and (b) half of us were the Dún Laoghaire perennial arty crowd. Pam cleverly worked out that a good way to meet everybody's interests was to offer, *before* the soup at six o'clock – an afternoon copper-enamelling class. Was there no end to the woman's talents?

Back when this whole summer Bible-distribution programme began, one of the organisers, a medical student, wrote to me, 'If you have any babies you want delivered just send them up here for first class attention.' Of course, he was only joking and, as medical students will tell you, their joking is merciless. But then, you see, we were all students. It was a student movement - indeed much of it was a teenage movement - happening right under the nose of 1960s Ireland. That's probably the reason it was left largely undocumented. Even though there were 170 of us involved in this sea change at any one time, official 1960s Ireland took no notice. They certainly weren't bowled over by our movement's not-very-snappy name 'Gospel Literature Distribution'.

So far, this business of trusting the Jesus of the Bible was fine for those summers and half the winters. But for the many of us who aspired to be grown-up people one day, one big question remained – would it work?

CHAPTER 6

THE POLITICAL DISCUSSION SOCIETY

Trinity College and I parted company in July 1970, amicably enough – I with a microbiology degree and they with no regrets. On graduation day I wore the obligatory suit but inside my sombre-coloured footwear I wore white socks, just to make the point (to myself), 'I'm not quite what it appears; I'm a missionary inside, like I told the tutor four years ago.' The next day I headed back to Galway, the cultural centre of gravity of Ireland. I looked for a job at the university and quite soon they offered me one which was 'still being sketched out'.

They were involved in a new fish farm on Inis Oírr, one of the Aran islands, and needed somebody to regularly measure the fish. The successful candidate would spend a week per month on the island and the other three weeks in Galway. Just as I was getting ready to say, 'I'm your man,' they said, 'Oops, no, we miscalculated. It's *three* weeks per month on the island with the fish and *one* week back at the university.' Well, much as I liked fish (eating them anyway) and much as I regarded the Aran islanders with some awe, I was content to spend my whole month in Galway city.

Before long I was offered a research job by Dr James Houghton of the Microbiology department. The project's overall grand plan was to develop food supplies for the 21st century by limiting the growth of algae in our rivers and waterways and, instead, getting it to grow in more suitable places where it could be harvested (like the Atlantic). My part of that plan was to guard the university's stock of blue-green algae in the meantime. I guarded them like a she-wolf. Of course, in order to prove myself as a researcher I needed to do the odd bit of experimenting and submit it for publication, hopefully cementing my name (and that of the head of department) in the annals of science for all time. The British Journal of Mycology didn't see it this way and 'declined' to publish it – they thought I'd said nothing new. Apparently they knew more about algae than I did. But the Micro department gave me a happy year.

As the year progressed I met up with a couple of other people at University College Galway ('UCG'[3]) who shared my hankerings after perusing the Bible and its implications. We also found students who often declared themselves 'sick to the back teeth with Christianity', so we decided it was time to try an experiment. Would students

---

3   Later 'National University of Ireland Galway', later again 'University of Galway'.

be attracted to discuss the big things of life if they were presented to them in ordinary English? Spurred on by an idea we picked up from students in Spain, we wrote a 'Christian manifesto', printed 1,700 copies and signed them *all*. It began 'God is not religious, God is not old, God likes people...' and so on. We delivered them in person to first and second-year students in lecture halls just before lectures began. No movement was started, nobody rushed up to co-sign the manifesto but we began to run into people who had seen it and thought maybe the Bible was worth one last try for relevance, before it was junked.

Fr Tom Kyne, the chaplain, commended us for a gallant attempt but warned me that eventually the 'soporific air of University College Galway' would get me. To correlate with the manifesto, we wrote out, on a very long sheet of blank newsprint, the entire text of the New Testament book of 'Romans' and secured it on the grass outside the Quadrangle at the university entrance. One of us showed each potential reader where to start and another chatted with them when they had got through it. A medical student friend from Dublin, Ronald Grainger, came to sing Christian folk songs on his twelve-string guitar while people read.

The next month we thought we would have another try. It would be a public meeting – not *our* public meeting but we would provide a good speaker for a college society, the 'Political Discussion Society'. UCG was fiercely proud of the non-partisan nature of its charter so there couldn't be religious or political societies but a Political *Discussion* Society was okay. The society officers took to the idea like a duck to water and the day came when we sat down to an introductory meal in the Skeffington Arms hotel with Dr David Gooding of Queen's University, Belfast who had agreed to speak for us on 'Spiritual Revolution in Franco's Spain'.

Working my way through oysters in white wine at the society's expense (I still prefer fish) we briefed Dr Gooding on the talk which was supposed to tell the story behind those Spanish students who gave us the manifesto idea. I was worried too that although the title said 'spiritual revolution' a good percentage of the 150 who eventually turned up would want more information on Franco than Jesus. As it turned out, everybody was satisfied and we announced that the next morning, a Saturday, we would return to a lecture hall, the college's grandly titled 'Greek Hall', for a seminar on Bible study also given by Dr Gooding.

Saturday arrived but the people didn't – at least not 150 of them. About a dozen of us packed into a hall built for 200 and after an hour or so adjourned for coffee to the flat in 12 Dominick Street where I lived with a couple of new friends. But what this dozen lacked in quantity they surely made up for in quality, because they simply wouldn't go away. Some of them turned up again on Sunday and it was then decided that a weekly Bible study group was in order. The group would comprise a doctor, a Commerce student (Frank Mulloy, who will still adjourn for coffee any time), myself, Ben (who was studying for the Dominican priesthood) and Ronnie who, had he been working, would have worked in Palmer's Mill in Nun's Island.

We had a 'deal' that in our winter of studying the Gospel of Luke we would always be open to 'do' what it said as well as read it. But laying yourself open to Bible influences like that has inevitable implications. Each of us in the group began to see items in Luke's gospel that called for putting into practice. Like how we used our money. At first we snorted, 'Ara, that's for those who have money!' Only to find that these were guidelines for us too, who had little. Guidelines also about personal relationships – which looked like they had been specially programmed in for my benefit, since I had just become engaged to that most beautiful girl in the world, Pam Serdahl, still working back in Dublin.

For Frank this study had different implications. The further we got into it, he began to fear that the text of the Gospel would drag him to a conclusion he didn't like one bit. As we covered case after case of Jesus forgiving sins, Frank felt the growing discomfort of knowing in his heart of hearts, that he had never been forgiven. Now there are few things that can cause such a feeling of acid in your insides as feeling unforgiven. Which is not to say that Frank had something awful to be forgiven for. In fact, something awful might have been more dramatic and easier to deal with. It was just the accumulated weight of being an ordinary nice guy for too many years without ever taking on God's offer of forgiveness for that endemic tendency to sin that makes monkeys of us all.

By Christmas this question had become somewhat of a fixation for Frank. New Year saw him put renewed zeal into his normally exemplary religious observance. He was going to work this thing out once and for all. Sometimes he wished he could work on it all day – and, in the end, that was what decided him to join me and some friends to take a bike trip from Dublin to Donegal and back for the Easter holidays. For ten glorious days he could cycle and think in the solitude of the Irish countryside, in the company of other searchers, and the companionship of his bike. Frank was of solid Westport stock and had taken care to bring his gents' black bicycle to college. Frank actually used the little leather pouch behind the saddle to carry tools in (I had always wondered what was in those pouches). He never saw the sense in walking or taking the bus even if the weather was filthy. He just hermetically sealed himself in the classical biker's oilskins.

Once in a blue moon we seem to get warm weather for precisely the Easter period. It appeared that we were in one of those years as we set out from Sallynoggin, picked up the odd latecomers at Trinity College front gate and pointed our noses towards Balbriggan. We arranged to stay in the An Oige hostel (then at Port Oriel) in Co. Louth which felt like a prodigious cycling distance on the day but looks sheepishly short on the map. Apart from the Galway contingent the party of a dozen or so included Vinnie, another inveterate cyclist, who was so balanced on a bike he could steer another empty one alongside with his free hand. Canice, also from Dublin, had come on his motorbike so he could scout out the road ahead and if necessary go back to assist tail-enders. The motorbike was a recent acquisition and I think the power went to his head. If we cycled 300 miles, Canice surely did over 500.

The level of spiritual commitment in the group was mixed. Everyone was happy for us to read a short Scripture passage night and morning and nobody objected to some of the group who had planned to distribute leaflets entitled 'Revolution of Love', on the occasions when we passed through civilisation. Frank volunteered to carry the few hundred bright yellow leaflets in his panier bag and guess who the British army chose to search as the line of bicycles crawled over the border into Co. Armagh? The leaflet chronicled the hopeful effects of repentance and submission to Christ, but unfortunately had the word 'revolution' in its title. And unfortunately for Frank, he hadn't read it. Eventually the officer involved was convinced to let go of Frank and the leaflets by a small delegation whose sole unifying feature was that they had read 'Revolution of Love'. Of course, we let the officer keep a copy for himself.

The evening we got to Armagh Frank lay in his sleeping bag, doubtless reliving the Army's line-by-line scrutiny of 'Revolution' and also mulling over the Bible passage we had just studied. Our daily dose had moved on through to Paul's letter to the Ephesians where we had read, 'It is by grace you have been saved, through faith – and this is not from yourselves, it is the gift of God – not by works, so that no one can boast.'

The next day, Aughnacloy, Ballygawley and Omagh moved slowly and deliberately under Frank's sturdy black steed. You get time to think on a bike. You see things you would never see from a car, like dead animals – crows, sheep, a horse and even a fox. You get a good feeling of 'paying your way' with physical energy for every mile. There is sometimes the odd sensation of having to cycle unusually hard against no appreciable incline and no wind that you can feel. And you think, especially if something is bugging you like Ephesians was bugging Frank.

Our County Tyrone stop was organised by my parents in Strabane but when the party lunged forward into sunny Donegal the next day I was not amongst them because Pam Serdahl had arrived to stay with my parents and I found a dozen good reasons to forego the Donegal loop of the journey. Sure, I'd seen Donegal before.

Three days later they picked me up with a cheery disdain and we once again scared the honest road-users of counties Tyrone and Armagh with our makeshift cycling caravan. Frank and I fell to talking away the now-familiar miles. That letter to the Ephesians was against his whole personal philosophy. He had always believed in doing his bit to win God's forgiveness. Forgiveness in Ephesians appeared cheap at first sight. 'It is not the result of your own efforts, but God's gift' is what got Frank. A funny arrangement – how could God save us for free? Surely then you could go out and paint the town red and still be forgiven! On the way through Armagh for the second time a light finally went on ... in Frank's head. Careful examination of Ephesians showed there was plenty of room for his good works ('He has created us for a life of good deeds' Paul writes) but only *after* you have taken God's forgiveness at face value and said, 'Thank you'.

Ben, one of the more athletic cyclists, asked him if he'd ever said, 'Thank you' to God like that. No, he didn't think he had. 'Any reason you wouldn't want to say it now?' No.

Frank said, 'Thank you,' and we set off for County Monaghan. Now there was no lighter bike than Frank's. It had taken five months to find that forgiveness. And Frank's was the only bike without gears. To this day Frank looks back on that bike trip as 'a major turning point' in his life. It would be good to be able to say that a lot of other Galway students made such a turn in 1971. They didn't. But that never stopped Frank's onward momentum. Like his heavy bike, now that he'd built up a bit of speed, he would turn out to be a tried and trusted rep for Christ in UCG.

CHAPTER 7

CROXON AND CO

The Galway to Dublin romance between Pam and me was only slightly facilitated by phone calls. I was no good on the phone. She would write gushing letters on pastel-coloured onion-skin paper (I still have them) and I would try and reply by calling her at work from a Galway street phone box, the time – and money – ticking by. We had less time and money to spend on travel to see each other but, every time we did, my fascination with her family grew. I had never met them. Her parents were divorced. That's always sad, but she was on good terms with both of them. Her father, Earl Serdahl, was an engineer who had since been re-married and divorced again. He would later go on to marry a third time. Nice chap, but not really the model we wanted to follow.

Everything about Pam's mother was new to me, starting with her name, 'Boo'. She was born 'Beulah' Williams. She lost the 'Beulah' to 'Boo' – easier for a child to say. But when we went to look for why she was 'Williams', unravelling that mystery was like reading an unlikely Western paperback. Boo's father, George Williams, was a lawman, deputy to the sheriff of San Benito County in Northern California. The sheriff was Boo's grandfather, Jeremiah Croxon – they kept the law in the family.

We don't know much about George's original circumstances, except that they were meagre. When Sheriff Croxon found him, he took pity on him, raised him as his son, and gave him a job. What better job than to be his own deputy? While Croxon was out there fighting baddies, all George had to do was stay in the office and keep the accounts. So firm was their bond that Jeremiah Croxon smiled when George's relationship with Jeremiah's daughter, Meta, blossomed into marriage and they set up home in Hollister (no, not that Hollister but the real one in California).

It was into that law-abiding family that Boo and her sister Betty were born. However, when Boo was five years old, on the night before the annual county audit, her father disappeared off the face of the earth, as did $6,000 belonging to the county. To be precise, George was off the face of North America – in South America. Sheriff Croxon had to break this news to his tearful daughter. This would be a disaster in any family's record. What would Jeremiah do next?

I am proud to say that I belong, however tentatively, to a family tree that has Jeremiah Croxon in it. Because, once he had George Williams trailed to the Panama Canal Zone, he trusted no one but himself to lay hands on George and so went down to Panama himself and brought him back to face normal justice in California. But what about the $6,000? The newspaper recorded that 'Croxon gave his life savings to make good the shortage.'[4]

Everything had to start over again – Jeremiah's finances, Meta's family life, the sheriff's reputation. And Boo's vision of a father. Meta took a cruise to straighten out her head and heart. Which is where she met her new husband, Jack Logan, the only father Boo would ever remember and a more stable man you couldn't find. Guess what? – he was another policeman, this time a California Highway Patrolman.

In his home town of Hollister, Jeremiah acquired the nickname 'Golden Rule Croxon'. He had the reputation of never having lost a prisoner out of his custody, and went on being elected sheriff until he was the oldest living sheriff in the world.

The Hollister house is still standing on a plot of land with a barn at the back. Recently, on a visit to the town, Pam and I decided to peek inside the barn. It was packed full of possessions stored by the five generations since the famous sheriff. In a dark corner, under a dusty pile of books we noticed a Bible, a real 'Holy Bible' in serious black leather. The page inside the back cover was covered with handwriting, declaring all the tenets of the Christian faith – a bit like a creed. At the end was written, 'My Testament, Jeremiah Croxon'.

---

4   San Bernardino County Sun, July 26, 1926

Now I understood why Pam was referring to our up-coming marriage as 'the first normal one on our side of the family in 100 years'. The next few months would be a good test of that prediction.

CHAPTER 8

WITNESS

I was still learning the ropes in UCG when I ran into an old friend of Pam's from County Clare, Sr Marie McNamara, walking down the street in Galway. She was the principal in St Joseph's Secondary School, Spanish Point and knew me fairly well. After we had chatted about what I was working at (so far, fish and algae) she said, 'There's a teacher lost in you. Do the 'Dip'.' What the university nowadays calls the 'Professional Master of Education' i.e. training teachers for secondary schools, was, back in the day, called the 'Higher Diploma in Education' or the 'Dip', for short.

Hence Marie's summary directive, 'Do the 'Dip'.' So, I did. I went straight to see Fr Hayden who was in charge of the college's Education department. He signed me up readily and sent me to see Mother Colombière at the Presentation Secondary girls' school (then on Presentation Road) to get 'hours'. To do the Dip you needed 'hours'. These were unpaid hours of teaching in a local school to develop your practical skills. It was the 21st November. I remember that because when I arrived at the Presentation convent they informed me that it was their feast day, the Feast of the Presentation, and I'd have to wait until Monday for an answer.

The whole thing was new to me – feasts, presentations, 'hours' – teaching itself for that matter. I still harbour a secret belief that I was so new to them that it would take them until Monday to work out how to give 'hours' to the first non-woman ever to work in the building. But somehow they managed. And somehow I managed to teach the prescribed course – a Leaving Cert biology module on human reproduction. The girls that I taught never showed as much as a flicker of wonder, amusement or amazement. No giggling, no anything. I guess they just thought, 'Has our education come down to this?'

I had almost forgotten that during the Dip I would undergo an unannounced on-site inspection. Until it happened. In a most unfortunate way. I went into the school one morning and found the designated inspector, a Jesuit priest, waiting for me. I was late. I was mortified. I tried not to be flustered. By this stage I was teaching the girls about crystallography. He sat at the back and took notes. I dutifully ploughed through my material. Class finished, girls dismissed, Jesuit still sitting there. 'I liked the way you developed that diagram of the crystal,' he commented. I gulped a subdued 'Thank you'. 'And the preparation notes the girls had'. 'Thanks,' again. Then he simply got up to leave. 'One more thing,' he said, Columbo-style, 'you were a little late.' Oops, now the cat was out of the bag. 'Purely human error, I take it?' 'Yes,

yes,' I agreed wholeheartedly, 'purely human error'. And, at that, he left. What a kind man.

I must confess that I now invested much less time in my Micro mates since I was doing the Dip, teaching in the Pres. and planning to get married. The lab guys were easy to get on with, a laugh a minute, and were growing increasingly curious about the Bible study in our place in Dominick Street.

Jimmy Clair, another Micro man, came into the lab one morning and announced to me that he and some friends would turn up at my place on Tuesday for 'one of these Bible Studies' whether I liked it or not. I turned up myself to find over half of the happy-go-lucky department eagerly awaiting my explanation of why on earth I paid so much attention to the Bible.

I was daunted by the openness of these hard-headed fellow-scientists whom I had come to respect. We landed on an agreed Bible passage that evening from the last book of the Bible, the book of Revelation. Why not? – it's already got a reputation as a spectacular book. We focussed our attention on the kind proposal from Jesus near the beginning of the book: 'Here I am! I stand at the door and knock. If anyone hears my voice and opens the door, I will come in and eat with that person, and they with me'. We spent the evening thinking backwards and forwards through the issue. Then after wolfing down our tea and biscuits, they left as suddenly as they came. I can understand that nobody wanted to break ranks and say, 'Right, sign me up', but the spell was broken in the lab and we felt comfortable talking about these issues after that. It wasn't long before one of the Micro students came back and asked how precisely she would go about making Christ welcome in her life and eventually ended up as a lodger in our house after Pam and I got married that summer!

It was the wedding of the year (it was for us anyway!). For more than many couples, it was a big deal for both of us. Pam often rightly points out that we could scarcely have been more different (I keep pointing out that, for starters, she was a girl!). Apart from the fact that I loved her, the clincher was that she had an inordinate desire to do whatever God wanted. That was something that had developed back in her school days.

Oakland, in the San Francisco Bay Area 90 miles north of Hollister, was where Pam's family made their home: Earl, Boo, Pam and her brothers, Eric and Chris. She remembers her parents as loving, competent, hard-working – and without so much as a whiff of religion, let alone overt Christian faith. When it came to high school, Pam attended a school in Castro Valley, also in the Bay Area, and it was there that her encounter with Christ took place. A girl in her year, Jane Rose, was going on a ski weekend and suggested that Pam join her. The Californians love it that you can ski in the morning and swim in the Pacific (if you wanted to) in the afternoon. A ski trip with Jane was hard to pass up.

Planned thinking time had been built into the weekend with someone providing meditations about the ultimate things in life and keeping a relationship with God central. Even when they're not planned, down times just happen anyway when you ski. Pam got to thinking and knew in herself that she needed to start up a relationship with God from scratch. The guy giving the reflections was helpful and gave Pam enough tips so she could say to God, 'I'd like to be forgiven and could we start off from here?' This was a path already taken by Jane so they had a new bond that kept them together.

Jane was a church-goer and so Pam did too. She wasn't long attending before the church concluded, 'We've got the makings of a proficient Sunday School teacher on our hands.' The next thing, Pam was teaching little kids about David and Goliath. The only fly in the ointment was that although Pam looked good and always acted more confident than she felt, she didn't have the years of Bible background that others had – not even as much as some of the children. Pam's integrity nudged her to make a radical move to catch up. She left her well-paid secretarial job at Lawrence Radiation Laboratory in Livermore, California and enrolled in Emmaus Bible School in Chicago.

Like all bittersweet partings, this was an affecting one for Pam's mother. Boo had happily caught up with God too – or rather he had caught up with her. Pam was as close as she would have to a heart-friend. As Pam was packing to leave, Boo said, 'I don't think you'll be back here again.' Mothers have some kind of extrasensory perception. She was right. Pam never lived in California again. Before long it was Donegal, Sligo and Galway that captured her. While in Chicago she heard about an opportunity to work in Christian literature distribution in Ireland and that catapulted her into the realm of thought where she could be a missionary. She wouldn't even have to learn Spanish! Somehow this criterion had repeatedly raised its head and she realised she didn't like learning Spanish in school. Spanish-speaking people yes, speaking Spanish, no.

Now she was 6,000 miles away, getting to know a guy who smelled like Dettol all the time because he was required to wash his hands in it before he left his place of work. Sometimes he seemed more animated about his beloved blue-green algae than about her – certainly on the phone.

At one point the planning of the wedding took a tricky turn because our funds were so low (they were almost below sea level). Indeed, when I told my mother that we were getting married she asked me, 'What *on*?' In her day you saved up and got married *on* £500 or *on* £1000 or whatever. I'd forgotten to do the saving up bit. It was one of those situations where you *either* invite the people who *have* to be at the wedding or you invite all your friends whom you *want* to be with – except that you don't feed them.

Pam came up with the radical proposal that we invite everybody we wanted and feed them just tea and cake. We reckoned that, since she was an American, people wouldn't know what to expect anyway. However, this brilliant idea didn't fly with the women Pam worked with in Dublin who said, 'Invite all your friends and we'll feed them a proper buffet lunch.' They were true to their word and fed our 200 friends and family in the cavernous church basement of Merrion Hall in Merrion Street after we got married in a little church in Dun Laoghaire.

You'd think getting married in a little church in Dun Laoghaire (by a Christian layman) would be simplicity itself. And that's what I thought – until it came to registering our intent to marry. The issue was that layman. Apparently marriages were solemnised by clergy of major denominations who also doubled as representatives of the state for this purpose. We weren't into the big denomination business so we also had to be recognised by a registrar for marriages.

First, weeks before, I had to proclaim to the registrar in Galway, in person, that we had the intent to wed. It wasn't difficult to find him. He'd just had a heart attack and was in Galway Regional Hospital. They gave me his ward number at Reception downstairs. I was admitted to his room, explained my request gently, not wanting to disturb his condition any further. 'Oh no!' he exclaimed, 'I knew this would happen when they put me in here!' He was such a fastidious civil servant that he had arranged for his big registration book to be placed in a cupboard in his hospital room. My job was to extract the big book from the cupboard, prop him up in bed and show him where to sign the record – all without inducing any more heart attacks in either of us.

That still left us with the quandary of how to get married by the layman, all the while needing the presence of a registrar on the day. To our everlasting relief we then found out that the Registrar General for Ireland was a member of that same little Dun Laoghaire church and was more than happy to become a guest at our wedding. So fear not, we're legally married! Of course, to become a guest you needed to be invited and for this we are forever grateful to Earl and Boo who put both their names to the invitations, despite the fact that they were long since divorced. Not only so, but they turned up in proper wedding couture and appeared in all the photographs – and all this during a time when divorce couldn't even be mentioned in our parliament since it was unconstitutional. It didn't officially exist. Earl and Boo did us proud and nobody ever noticed.

Our honeymoon in Jerusalem was done on a shoestring, like everything else. My wife's trust in my organising abilities was misplaced since I had never flown out of the country before. We travelled out on one-way student tickets, without hotel reservations but armed with a copy of *Israel on Ten Dollars a Day*. It worked out well, for a while. After a couple of weeks we began to think about getting back home and I climbed up the stairs to the Jerusalem office of the Israel student travel outfit to buy our return tickets, using the few shekels we had set aside for the purpose. 'Yes, we can sell you a ticket,' they said, 'but not for your wife.' 'Why not my wife?' I demanded, aghast. 'Spouses can't travel on student tickets from here like they do in Europe.' They wouldn't budge.

I went down to the street and explained the situation to Pam. 'We're going nowhere on the money we have left.' On the one hand we prayed. On the other hand she's as cool as a cucumber in a crisis and sallied forth into a regular travel agent's and put our case to the woman at the desk. 'The problem is, I'm not a student,' Pam explained. The woman had an attitude of 'You're not going to get stuck on your honeymoon – not on my watch you're not.' 'Were you ever a student?' she enquired. 'Once upon a time, in Chicago.' 'Did you have a student card?' 'Sure, I did.' 'Do you still have it?'

Thereupon, Pam dived into her handbag and found, right at the bottom, her old student card (never criticize the size of a woman's handbag). 'That will do.' said the pleasant agent and issued us tickets to Dublin at the student price – on Swissair. We were vastly relieved, but only a little bit vastly. The bungling member of our duo (me), who was in charge of logistics, still didn't have enough money to pay our hostel bill, including the days until the flight.

It fell to me to compose the telegram to Boo, still in Dublin, to wire us the $200 which would release us from our self-inflicted predicament. In the midst of all this we were walking down a narrow Jerusalem street and I spotted, in a cluttered shop window, a copy of the Bible in old Farsi. Having not quite got used to being married (and consulting on such decisions) I stepped right in and bought the book, much to my new wife's chagrin. It is a credit to her long-suffering that I still have that Bible.

You'd think I would have learned my lesson by now, but when we arrived in Galway the adorable little blue cottage on Newcastle Road on which I *thought* we had a contract, was now occupied by somebody else. We turned to a good doctor friend for help who said, 'I think I know of a bed here at Merlin Park Hospital.' Of course hospitals have beds, but this one was special. It was a single bed (out of use) that had been pushed into the library. 'Make sure you're out by seven in the morning when the cleaners come,' was his cheery final instruction.

The next day we signed for a flat share (with two loud nurses on rotating shifts) above Geoghegan's shop – then as now, a convenience store further up Newcastle Road from that lovely cottage. The nurses were called 'Concepta' and 'Assumpta'. So we were routinely woken in the middle of the night, as one or another of them came home, slamming the front door and shouting 'Cepta!' or 'Sumpta!'

When friends saw how the sensible Pam ended up with the likes of me, they murmured in a kindly, indulgent way that she had 'run away with me'. If only they knew the truth. I can see what they can't see – a daredevil woman who had enough fortitude to withstand such a couple of months, just to be a missionary with me. For it was I who ran away with her.

As soon as we set up home in Galway, Pam's appearing on the scene changed a lot of things. It was she who met a student called Margaret when the academic year began in the autumn of 1971. The Bible study had grown to ten and Margaret was a stalwart member. It wasn't just a Bible study any more. We were slowly becoming a little community in the college with a growing commitment to help each other. We suspected that Margaret was asking Christ to help her run her life.

Soon we found out that she was asking him for even bigger things – like helping her run her relationship with the rest of her dysfunctional family. She asked Pam to pray for this and the whole story tumbled out. Margaret's father was an alcoholic with a secure job. Her mother was trying to bring up a large family on a pittance, and failing. They all looked to Margaret, the eldest, to bail them out of trouble, wash and feed the kids, run the house and protect her mother from her father. No mean task for a seventeen year old. Now we would see if the gospel was indeed 'good news', relevant in such a family situation.

You can't avoid the fact that the Bible had a lot of dysfunctional families and some of those Biblical families looked awfully Irish. We watched for months as Margaret simply trusted God to help her hold the dying embers of her family together. One day she got a message that her mother had gone into hospital and we all started praying again as Margaret headed for home once more. Pam joined her to visit her mother, now in Ballinasloe Mental Hospital. Even the word 'Ballinasloe' was used by mothers to 'put a bit of *dacency*' on errant children as in, 'If you go on like that you'll have me in Ballinasloe!' Margaret explained to Pam what she had just pieced together herself. Her father had joined forces with the local doctor, a crony of his, to sign her mother into hospital so he could create a diversion to cover his drinking. It took two weeks to sort this out, by which time Margaret was plumbing depths of Biblical wisdom that she suddenly needed. But how to get her mother out again? Eventually, through some sympathetic hospital staff and visits to the priest at home, it was arranged. But now a gulf had opened in the family, that slowly widened as her parents grew apart.

When her mother finally left and went to set up home in Dublin it was Margaret again who held the family pieces together – by every power known to man, and by another less known. At the end of that incredible year what did Margaret do with her faith in God? She took time in a summer school on faith-sharing so she could help others.

I was glad to have Pam on side when we were introduced to Ida. She was a Dutch au pair who had suffered a bad car crash and ended up in the orthopaedic ward. In one way that was a good thing because it brought her into contact with a kind and sympathetic surgeon who also happened to be a passionate follower of Christ. His listening ear heard that she was estranged from her separated parents. Ida had sought meaning in travel, in occult prophecies and eventually settled for the security of a job in County Galway. Just being in hospital had opened a dangerous door in her mind as she discovered the oblivion of hospital drugs used in operations and began to depend on them. But her longing for acceptance dogged her every footstep and never found a resting place until the surgeon told her that since Jesus had died for her, he surely must love her more than anybody did. If she would only commit herself to Jesus he would heal her heart too.

Ida made that commitment and after she was released from hospital she became a twice-weekly occurrence at our flat on her days off. In a mixture of Dutch and English she became a keen student of the Bible. We were a little apprehensive that she would simply transfer from depending on chemicals to depending on us. Although we enjoyed her company we told her that most of all she would need to learn to trust God. Her leg did heal, and her heart too, but one day she said that she found that she had already reached a plateau in her life and she began to show signs of anxiety.

The father of her au pair family was experimenting in a current fad learned from RTE's *Late Late Show* – trying to contact the dead by electronics. Ida knew that the Bible speaks out quite plainly against this: 'Don't let them consult the spirits of the dead,' so she asked one of our group, Ben Mosher, and Pam and me to go out to their house and pray for her protection from evil, which we happily did. Before we prayed, Ben asked Ida, 'Have you done occult stuff yourself?' Slowly she said 'yes' and then began to list all the ways in which she had been spiritually compromised. These included the use of all kinds of magic charms. Then she added, 'Including I went to a fortune teller who predicted my life and gave me a ring that she said incantations over.'

Ben asked her if she was prepared to denounce these practices once and for all and break those ties with her old life, so Christ would be in charge of every corner of her heart. Ida renounced each item on her list out loud, asked God to forgive her for each and then asked him to clean her life out. Each of us prayed and soon Ida was laughing with a feeling of freedom. After the rest of us went home she flushed that fortune-telling ring well and truly down the toilet.

In a couple of months Ida's father got in touch with her and suggested that she return to Majorca, where he lived, and after winding up her affairs in Galway, she left town for Palma – but not before 'going public' about her new-found faith. Ida is a strong-minded person and her chosen way to do that was to be baptised in public to show she had crossed the line to a new allegiance to Christ.

She chose me to do the baptising. The word got out (after all, it was public) and the morning came where I gladly baptised Ida in the Corrib river, just beside the Salmon Weir Bridge. You couldn't miss it – it's opposite the Cathedral. Not only did the *Connacht Tribune* newspaper arrive to take photographs but quite a few Galway mothers arrived – when they heard that a girl was going to be baptised they immediately thought it was going to be a *baby* girl, which had understandably given them some concern. The *Tribune* gave it front page treatment two days later: 'Christians, as they call themselves, follow the Bible and meet with each other to read it and worship Christ.'[5] Accurate enough, although not rocket-science.

Meanwhile, back at the ranch, we too were learning 'family' things in double quick time. We were pregnant.

---

5   Connacht Tribune, November 19, 1971

CHAPTER 9

SIOBHÁN

Much as I wanted to be with Pam when the baby was born, I ended up in bed with bronchitis at the time. Ben Mosher and his family kindly took me to stay with them in their house in Merlin Park on the Dublin Road. So when the phone rang to say that the great moment was arriving, I hastily dressed and was bundled into the Regional Hospital waiting room. A whole generation of Galway fathers knew the nondescript walls of that room. But the doctor wanted to see me as soon as I came in.

He was young – only qualified a couple of years. I was immediately put off by something too solemn in the look of him. He got around to it quickly. 'Mr. Wilson, I'm afraid we have some bad news for you. Your wife has given birth to a baby girl – but she was born with a difficult condition – it's called "spina bifida". Basically what it means is…' At this point I was staring straight through this guy's head – hearing him but not hearing him. His helpful and sympathetic explanation of spina bifida was tucked into my memory somewhere for future retrieval, but all I wanted to do was see Pam. So the doctor brought me to the recovery room right away and we walked as fast as decorum would allow.

It struck me to ask him, 'But can this condition be corrected?', 'Well some cases are mild but I'm afraid…' He was 'afraid' again. This wasn't a mild case. 'There is an operation which can close over the lesion in the spine, and later the pressure on the brain can be relieved with another operation. I have to tell you, she might not survive the operations. And, if she did – there is nothing we can do to reverse the condition. You see, the damage is already done.'

By this time I was at Pam's bedside. We fell into each others' arms, and my pride in her bearing my child was none the less for the baby's condition – all the more, in fact, because her attitude was so collected. We prayed for wisdom and talked together, for by now the doctor had given us a choice. Did we want to proceed with the operations? The instant response of both of us was – 'Do all you can do, doctor.'

It's like being in a car crash. You get out and check that 'nobody is seriously hurt.' Then you see if the vehicles are 'still drivable.' Then you see if we can 'get it home anyway, and then we'll work on fixing it up.' Only over the next few hours did it slowly dawn that somebody was 'seriously hurt' and we wouldn't 'get her home anyway.' By that time I had seen Siobhán, for so she was called, in intensive care, and gone back out to Mosher's. I also got more medical opinion – this time not so hopeful about an operation, nor Siobhán's prognosis.

After teatime I had begun to conclude that we had made the wrong decision, and stumbled into the Regional to talk and pray with Pam again. What a wife! The passing of the day and our earnest conversation together brought us to one mind and the conclusion not to proceed with the operation that evening. But things were already in preparation, and the decision wasn't made any easier when the surgeon told us he even had students lined up in the theatre to see the operation because it was such an unusual case. He called me over to the theatre to sign our decision on paper. I have often wondered what he did with the paper. Did he throw it in the waste paper basket when I left? Was it just to make us think seriously? Did he keep it in our file in case there were any questions later on? Indeed, if we had that day to live over again now, with hindsight and knowing so much more about spina bifida and what was medically going on, would we make a different decision?

I thanked the medical staff the best I knew how, checked on Pam who was by this time asleep, went home and wrote in my diary a line from the book of Job which we had recently studied: 'The Lord gave and now he has taken away. May his name be praised.' The date was Valentine's Day.

I returned to my bronchitis and went to bed. It seemed like I went to bed a lot for the next two or three days, but sleep was fitful and sporadic. I kept wakening up with the vivid mental image of Siobhán and her deformity. I prayed to God to take this nightmare away. He didn't. After three days of this I realised that although I had prayed prayers before, during and after the baby's birth, I had not 'talked straight' to God about the central problem. On that Friday morning I cried, 'O God, the baby is deformed!' and went to sleep. He heard me. Now we were on speaking terms again.

Siobhán was moved to the fever hospital where she was looked after with fanatic loyalty by the nuns there for the rest of her short life. Pam gathered strength back in the ward, I recovered and soon we were back home in Beechmount Road trying to reassemble our lives. I was teaching, by this time, in the Holy Rosary Secondary School in Mountbellew, courtesy of the Sisters of the Christian Retreat, and Pam was receiving family and kind visitors of all sorts. It's tough on any woman to leave the maternity ward without her baby. She has to contend with all the things that people say to her and with all the people who don't know what to say. Pam told people simply that we were very sad but that we trusted God because we already knew that he loved us.

After a week or so we gathered in the hospital with a few friends and asked God to heal Siobhán. He chose not to, and again we knew that at least we had communicated to him exactly what our desires were.

On Monday morning, the 12th of March, I was called out of a maths class to take a phone call I had awaited for 26 days – from Pam to say that Siobhán was dead. She borrowed a friend's Morris Traveller (a small Morris

Minor Estate car) and came out to Mountbellew to pick me up. We drove back to Galway slowly. On the way we stopped to look over a fence at the new season's lambs and think.

I don't know why I hadn't thought of funeral arrangements before, but I hadn't. It's funny – you cling on to life, even irrationally, while it's still there. We drove out to the big cemetery in Bohermore which is distinguished by its two chapels, one at either end, one for Catholic services, one for Protestants. The caretaker explained that the religious division went further – to the extent that the whole cemetery was arranged with a Protestant section and a Catholic section. The idea of such tribal separation was a step too far for me and I asked if there were any middle ground. He said, 'No,' and showed me the line of demarcation. I asked if Siobhán could be buried under that line. 'No,' again.

We took our leave and I remembered that Walter Macken, in one of his historical novels (*The Scorching Wind*), mentions a cemetery up in Rahoon – on the other side of town, near where we lived in fact. Sure enough, it was still there and it had no such Catholic and Protestant arrangement.

I went down to Willie Conneely, the undertaker in Market Street, to order a small coffin, and he asked me if we wanted something fancy. I said that no, we didn't want a lot of extra trappings because, from the best we could gather from the Bible, the baby was safe in heaven with God and no religious trimmings at this point would help her. I launched into an explanation of the Biblical account of King David's statement when his infant died– 'I shall go to him, but he will not return to me,' only to find Willie weeping. 'Isn't it a crazy thing,' he said, 'that you come in here to buy a coffin and I end up weeping, but I would love to have this confidence you have that you will go to be with God.' I explained that my confidence stemmed from the fact of Jesus taking my Hell for me on the cross, and eventually left his Dickensian shop with a beautiful simple white coffin and Willie much happier.

The Corporation office in Dominick Street sold me a plot in Rahoon Cemetery, and after painstakingly filling out the form 'Wilson K5/10' asked me who would 'officiate' at the funeral. As it happened we had chosen to ask a few friends to join us in singing, Bible reading and prayer, but nobody in particular was going to 'officiate.' I explained to the Corpo man that we were burying this child's body to await the resurrection when Jesus comes back and that meanwhile she was being well taken care of in heaven. He listened in a daze of disbelief, thanked me most sincerely and returned to his desk.

In Rahoon I read out, from the last page of the Bible, the same beautiful words we had sent to *The Irish Times*, 'Come Lord Jesus!' We thanked God for Siobhán's life, and Joe Noble, a good friend who drove a taxi in town, sang the song, 'O the deep, deep love of Jesus'. No big audience – just family like my parents, friends like Anna and Susan, and neighbours like Joe and Evelyn. Anna came round later to say that standing there that afternoon she had seen enough spiritual reality to help her decide to invite Christ into her life too. 'You see,' she said, 'For all the times I've been to Rahoon Cemetery, I've never sung in it before.'

CHAPTER 10

BECOMING A PERMANENT FEATURE

It was nuns who had given me my first break in teaching, and my second, and had cared for Siobhán with such compassion. Very shortly thereafter it was nuns again, this time unsettling our composure.

'Sister and I have a little announcement to make,' said one of the two sweet, religious ladies sitting so primly in our front room.

'Six weeks ago, when you challenged us to take our relationship with Christ to a personal level we both went away and did just that. But we thought we'd better not tell yet, to see would it work. In this six weeks we saw something happen we'd only heard about before and now we think it's time to tell. You see, when Pam was in the hospital we went down to see her, to bring her comfort, but when we got there it was she who encouraged us. We'd heard about joy in the midst of sorrow. Now we've seen it and we want our lives to be different too.'

'Yes,' said the other sister (the little announcement wasn't over yet), 'and when I went home the first thing I did was to burn the dirty magazines I kept in my room.'

That was a showstopper. We gasped in disbelief and seeing our minds boggling, Sister simply confirmed that it was so and prayed a simple prayer thanking God for forgiving her.

Now Beechmount Road was becoming a little hub of our spiritual co-op. Pam and I had decided to call our house 'Glyahawpfyl', an acronym for 'God loves you and has a wonderful plan for your life', earnestly hoping that someone would ask us what it meant. We made a sign for the front wall. Nobody ever asked. When we eventually left that house, we decided to tell the postman. He, like others, thought it looked 'vaguely Welsh'.

Maybe Frieda, who lived in the flats next door, had better sense in this business of encouraging people. Somehow we, and a good number of the artistically-minded students at UCG, seemed to gravitate to her place every so often in the evening. She is the heart and soul of good nature and you'd have thought she invented the word 'hospitality'.

She looked like she was 'born good' and she was interested in relating to Jesus, not only for forgiveness, but as a leader to follow in making one's mark in life. And she certainly made her mark. All were welcome in Frieda's: believers, prospective believers and pagans alike. Some of them went on to be Redemptorists and some went on to be ex-Redemptorists. It seemed like all we ever did there was sing, eat apple tart and drink (some tea, some cider – the tea was cheaper and didn't run out so fast).

Folk songs were in order ('Will ye gang to the highlands' was a favourite) and a few of us were writing songs to prove G. K. Chesterton wrong when he said of the 'Gaels' that 'all their wars are merry and all their songs are sad'.[6] We had a song about Bartimaeus, the blind man who met Jesus, to the tune of 'The Patriot Game' and we had Biblical advice on wisdom, from the book of James in the New Testament, to the tune of 'Báidín Fheilimí'. When you sing a song twenty times the words tend to stick in your head, the idea sticks in your heart, and with such companionable believers you just might grow up a bit.

By now it was becoming obvious to Pam and me that there would never be enough time to do all we'd like to do. I was teaching in East County Galway (a daily car-pool commute of 30 miles each way) and I often felt like the proverbial one-armed paper-hanger. For example, when I had a key meeting with some student activist friends in Blackrock in Dublin how could I get there, spend the evening and teach again the next day?

The teachers in our car-pool came to the rescue. Their part was to race me to the Dublin train, which I caught at Attymon, directly after school. And the part played by Easons' newspaper van was to bring me back to Galway by seven in the morning, lying in a pile of newspapers which was added to at Dublin airport by the Irish editions of the English papers. OK – I learned a lot

6   Ballad of the White Horse, book ii, Methuen, London 1911.

about transport but I couldn't go on living like that.

The new term brought with it a hard choice. Would I take a further step on the wild side and leave teaching so we could spend our whole time engaging with students about life's enormous issues? One single sea change made it easier – we had company, in the form of some like-minded friends who had offered to come and make a little team with us. They had been trained by Campus Crusade for Christ (now called 'Agapé'). Again, they were non-denominational. Again, we would stay simple. It was a deal we couldn't afford to miss – so we took it.

Although we looked forward to this with great relish, one thing had yet to be overcome. I loved what I was already doing (teaching). I loved the children and I liked the school. Was it worth leaving those dozens of fresh-faced East Galway kids for the rough and tumble of university activism? I was impressed by some of Jesus' teachings which seemed to be right to the point and I noted them in my diary. 'If one of you is planning to build a tower, he sits down first and works out what it will cost, to see if he has enough money to finish the job.' I wrote to my parents and suggested we all get together for a weekend in a guesthouse in County Wicklow and discuss this proposed move. My parents gave wise advice and were most supportive of the idea of us taking up such work as a life-long career.

The die was cast. Sister Dympna, the head teacher in Mountbellew, arranged a mutually agreeable deadline for my leaving and asked me, 'Just what exactly will you tell these students at the university?' I explained the concept of coming to know the Lord in a personal way. We spent an hour and a half discussing the relevant Bible passages and at the end she said, 'Well, Mr Wilson, I hope you tell this to the others.' 'You mean the teachers?' I asked. 'The children, too,' said Sister Dympna. I had always had a personal rule that when I was being paid to teach the children chemistry, chemistry is what they would get. So I checked that she really wanted me to use the chemistry time, or biology or maths, to teach these principles from the Bible.

She gave the go-ahead and that started my last and maybe my best month in the Holy Rosary College. I gave each class one session on 'The Four Spiritual Laws'. This was not as strange as it might seem because it was not unusual in a Science class for me to say, 'The subject of today's class has implications which are moral and spiritual and which we won't go into today because they are beyond the scope of this course,' (this could be, for example, about human reproduction or nuclear power).

This opened the way for me to begin these swan-song classes, 'Just as there are physical laws that govern the physical universe, so there are spiritual laws that govern our relationship with God.' The pupils regarded this as perfectly logical and for each class I drew a diagram on the blackboard demonstrating what it means to have Christ come in to take control of one's life.

I felt I had fulfilled a certain obligation to the students of Mountbellew, which might never have happened without any change in my career, and my last obstacle to that change was gone. Something I hadn't anticipated was that I would meet many of these kids again when they were students at UCG – they were the only ones who ever called me 'Mr Wilson'!

Strange as it may seem – the fatefulness of making this decision overshadowed the perfectly obvious question of how we were going to manage financially. It was all the more affirming when some friends and people I had known as fellow-students from my college days put together enough money to hold our bodies and souls together. We could never grow fat on such a capped salary (still haven't!), but it met our needs.

Rather than just wait around for students to seek us out, we went to meet them. UCG sported a student common room, a pre-fab building affectionately known as 'Smokey Joe's' which was the main student hang-out area until new buildings arose. Which is not to say that Smokey Joe's was inferior to the new concrete set-up. Indeed, the Boomtown Rats played Smokey Joe's, at 50 pence admission, under the benign eye of the common room manager Ollie Jennings, surely the youngest (and at that price the most successful) impresario in Ireland.

Now, during the day in Smokey Joe's there were two things. One was smoke and the other was no room. The tables were completely full of the best developed card schools in Galway and the corners were completely full of students eating furtive lunches. To meet this situation we developed the 'chair method' which was simplicity itself. You just procured a chair from the stack behind the door, went up to a card table, put down your chair in a crevice between the bodies and said, 'My name is Stephen and this is my friend David and we are talking to everybody in college about Jesus of Nazareth. Would you like to talk now or would you prefer to make an appointment?' (putting a chair in a crevice was the normally accepted way you joined a table).

As often as not, the tableful of card sharks would opt to go right ahead and talk to us on the spot, since who in his right mind wants to bother with an appointment? So we would give each one a copy of the 'Four Spiritual Laws' in a booklet format and read through it with them explaining each point. Some argued, some agreed, some appeared to sleep right through until we asked them what they thought about it. They would wake up with a jolt and we would have to backtrack to the beginning again.

It was brash, it was crazy, it took hours, it drained emotional energy, but we made friends for life there. Just before the holidays, on a day when the common room seemed to be admitting particularly heavy traffic, we met a student, Martin, who was selling tickets for the Geography Society Christmas party. He both talked *and* made an appointment to have dinner in a few days with our team-mates, the McGirr family. By Christmas, Martin's spiritual quest had changed from looking for the source of truth to plumbing its depths which became a life-long pursuit. It was like the change from prospecting for water to drilling and drinking it.

An old friend in the administration of the University kept asking me when I was going to get a 'real' job. I had never been very successful in explaining to him the satisfaction of seeing deep change in the lives of men and women. But in time, after he had gone up the pay scale a few notches, bought his house and got tired of being nouveau riche, he took me to the restaurant one day for coffee and said, 'I would give anything to swop jobs with you.'

Not all conversations in Smokey Joe's were sweetness and light. Like the guy who said to me (at one of those tables for six) 'No! I won't let you go on with what you have to say until you can answer me this one simple question. How come so many Israelites left Egypt and no Egyptian ever recorded the fact?' Only one fellow was asking the question but five were watching. Mostly they were watching me. And I was stumped. I don't like to be caught out on the same question twice so now it was homework time for me and I needed to say so. 'I'll come back and talk to you,' I said, 'but not until I find out the answer. Expect me.' Being stopped in your tracks with a short sharp shock is good for you once in a while. And anyway – how come no Egyptian ever recorded it? Homework time indeed.

The coffee shop next door, 'Ma Creaven's', named after its careful proprietor, gave me a temporary change of atmosphere (higher humidity) and engaged my mind on other issues. This was where a few socially-conscious student opinion-makers held court and asked questions like: 'Why do you have to be a Christian to do good? Why can't we just do good anyway?' One girl was very much into concrete help for others, as everyone should be, and challenged us to help her campaign to improve the central heating system in the flats in Rahoon. This apparently banal issue (unless, of course, you actually lived in Rahoon) was the *cause celebre* in Galway that year. You couldn't turn the central heating off and one councillor, a darling of the newspapers, had described the flats as a 'banana republic'. 'What do you mean "improve" the system?' we said. 'Make it better, silly,' she replied. 'But making anything "better" depends on your definition of good and that ultimately depends on the character of God – in whom you don't believe. Anyway, why make it better?'

'For the people who live there. Don't you care about the people?'

'Why are people important?'

'They just are.'

'You mean you don't know why people are important?'

'Go on then – you tell me why they're important.'

'Because they are made in the image of God. We're right beside you in helping people, except we have a reason.'

Reasons, reasons, reasons. Nobody ever came into the Kingdom of God just by reason. But few came in from Ma Creaven's without a decent brush with 'reason' en route. Going over the intellectual basis of the faith sometimes isn't too exciting. A lot of tea-times I went home with my head buzzing with three hours of debate and very little to show for it, at least in the short term.

I learned a lesson about the long-term effects of our philosophy from a fellow in a far-left political society in college (a society with an unofficial existence). Their central committee had broken up, allegedly from disagreement over the war between East and West Pakistan – about which different committee members took different sides. Later he told us that another issue had divided them. They had always had the monopoly in UCG on the philosophy of the future – which was basically dialectic materialism. But since a few students were now actively promoting a Biblical position on the future ('Jesus will come back again') there was suddenly a new contender for their cherished philosophical niche in the student mind. One of their officers confided to me that the pressure of this new alternative view of the future helped to put their society out of business.

But, back to Egypt. When I remembered the answer I couldn't wait to get back to the common room. My man was sitting as if he hadn't moved during the intervening two weeks.

'I've found the writings of an Egyptian prince which give a detailed chronicle of thousands of Israelites leaving Egypt,' I announced.

'Oh, who?'

'Moses.'

'Ah, but that's in the Bible. I don't believe the Bible!'

'So your problem isn't with the Israelites – you want to fly in the face of some of the best scholarship and then count your own opinion superior.'

'Maybe.'

His opinion didn't change but we got to return to the conversation we had started on day one. I left it there. The other lads were still watching and listening but saying nothing. I would have counted the whole episode as fragrance wasted on the desert air if one of the five, Pat Shanahan from Shantalla, near our house, had not come to me later to say that he was now trusting in a personal God and was going to study this properly in an academic course.

The college, in its wisdom, now installed tables and chairs in the Concourse in the new science building. The tables were low and the chairs, in sets of four, did not face into the table but at right angles to it. Once you sunk into this canvas bucket seat, conversation with your table partners was only possible if you were a contortionist or literally 'laid back'. The miracle is that the student populace did learn to talk like this and Tom was one of the best. Born in Nigeria of Irish parents and educated in Glenstal, Tom was best known in college for his interest in the stage. He had played in the well-received Dramsoc production of Ibsen's 'Hedda Gabler' that spring. A lovable, incurable romantic, he had ended up in the science faculty. I once met him while he was visiting a lady friend with a beautiful selection of four-foot long weeds which he had picked from the surrounding fields.

Who can resist such a scientist?

Tom had genuine difficulties with the evidence for the Christian faith. His debate with us, in the privacy of the Concourse, was because he wanted to know the facts, unlike others whose motivation was to escape the moral implications of the Bible. One thing that bothered Tom was the resurrection of Jesus since he had deduced, quite correctly, that if the resurrection facts were weak then the whole Christian edifice was built on shaky ground. Tip Killingsworth, one of Tom's best friends, lent him a copy of McDowell's *Evidence That Demands a Verdict*, which documents historical evidences for the resurrection.

He returned it after two weeks without reading it but highly impressed that it was over 300 pages long! I don't know what he had been expecting. Later he perused the New Testament and other history to check that Jesus was really dead on the cross. The evidence said, 'Yes'. He checked the burial, the records of the empty tomb, the appearing of Jesus to disciples. So far, so good. The more he looked into them the more the story held. The documents even told you eye-witness accounts of what Jesus had for breakfast. The simple changes in the disciples' outlook were convincing, almost mundane. The time was coming, and Tom knew it, for a lull in the research so his personal commitment to Christ as his Master could catch up with his academic reasons. That lull came and Christ was soon in charge of UCG's most winsome, poetic, actor-scientist.

Just reviewing the evidence wasn't good enough for some students. I lunched with one student who chatted affably enough as we proceeded through the same information about Jesus' resurrection. But as the implications in his own life became clear to him he eventually got angry and stood up shouting at me, 'Don't give me this Son of God stuff!' He threw down his knife and fork, which would have stuck in the table had it not been Formica-top, and stormed out leaving half his food.

From early days it became obvious that our day-to-day conversations would need to be informed and undergirded by serious study. We invited various scholars to come together and teach an annual summer school, the 'Institute of Biblical Studies'. This started in UCG in 1974 (a session best remembered for the fact that the college canteen stayed open an extra two weeks for us and produced over 300 kilos of chips in that period!).

By 1980 the Institute was being held in University College Dublin and we had benefited from the teaching of lecturers from as far afield as Ulster University (Coleraine), the Greek Department of Queen's University Belfast and the Department of Hebrew and Semitic languages in Liverpool University. But for learning practical apologetics I would gladly exchange a day at the Institute for an afternoon in Ma Creaven's.

I also discovered that leaving the rough and tumble of missionary life to its own devices (like dealing with chips by the kilo and ideas by the caseload) seemed to produce an admin jungle with tropical-style growth. Or maybe it was just me. I'll never forget the day the cavalry came over the hill and saved our bacon.

The cavalry in our case was my brother Myles and his wife Phyllis. They had followed the proceedings in UCG very carefully from the vantage point of good jobs in County Antrim. Myles was the production manager in a textile factory and Phyllis had started training as a nurse. I went to see them one day and we talked long into the evening about the exciting happenings in Galway and the exciting (and embarrassing) chaos that I was so capable of producing. I asked them if they could help. By the morning they had made a decision which utterly changed the trajectory of their lives. They decide to up sticks and come to the West to apply their redoubtable admin skills to our growing movement.

This meant that Myles needed to see his boss in order to hand in his notice. The boss said Myles's move was crazy but said a friendly goodbye. Six weeks later Myles and Phyllis were ensconced in Newcastle in Galway city and, as luck would have it, his old boss had lost his job because the company that owned the factory had gone bust. Maybe that old boss could have used Phyllis's skills in book-keeping because she marshalled our shambolic books into meticulous order. She is the kind of person who, when she's on holiday, wanders into office supply shops just to see what nice things they have on offer.

CHAPTER 11

HARBINGERS STREET THEATRE

Myles was a godsend because he was an inventive logistics expert (he still is). And that's what we needed when the *Harbingers Street Theatre* rolled into town. The Harbingers worked as an international touring company – I had encountered them in California. They mixed a dedication to quality drama with a commitment to communicating the Christian gospel via slapstick plays that got under your skin. It seemed like a winning combination to me and I said, 'Ireland loves the theatre!' and invited them to tour Ireland without asking them any further questions. This somewhat discombobulated their director and writer, Jeff Taylor. He was probably thinking, 'Maybe, just maybe, this eejit knows nothing about theatre.' He would have been right.

Mercifully, Myles then got involved in arranging the tour. Once the Harbingers arrived in Dublin, Jeff pointed out to Myles that the touring troupe was being accompanied by his two-year-old son who was being cared for by Jeff's wife Sue (one tough cookie). Where would they find a cot for him? Myles told him, 'Ireland has lots of babies so finding a cot won't be a problem.' In truth, he was thinking that we had a lot more complicated logistical problems to solve than that one.

So now we had eight actors, including a director with scripts in his head, some on paper, and one wife (pregnant as it happened) and a toddler. But no set for the play. Jeff came to our office on the fifth floor of 28 Westmoreland Street in Dublin to try and work out how to build the show's scenery. Myles came to the rescue again by handing Jeff the phonebook and suggesting he call the Abbey Theatre for help. The intrepid Jeff called and Joe Ellis, at that time the Abbey's production director, arranged for the Harbingers to get 25% off their bill at a local timber yard and the troupe started building scenery. We were in business.

Plan A was to perform their 30-minute play 'The Perfidious Temptation' on the Dining Hall steps in Trinity College but the college like to have notice of that sort of thing so the show got transferred, at a moment's notice, to the Junior Common Room above the college's Front Gate. The review in the *Evening Press* newspaper said, 'They acted out their "comedy-truth" drama with a single-mindedness and depth of concentration.'[7] That's a good thing because, being the Common Room, they had to compete with table soccer and snooker – a competition which was won by *The Perfidious Temptation*, according to the newspaper anyway.

---

7   Evening Press, February 1, 1979

One of the people most affected by the play was me. It told the serious side of the story of Adam and Eve from the book of Genesis in slapstick form (if you can hold all that in your head at the same time!). The actress who played Eve (Marilyn Mike) was so convincing in her portrayal of Eve experiencing labour pains that I forgot the table football, and indeed the whole Junior Common Room, as I was forced to think about the pathos visited on the world and womanhood in particular. Theatre does that to you. And the play survived to show again the next day at UCD Belfield.

Harbingers biggest hit must surely have been their show at Carysfort College in Blackrock, County Dublin – at that time a teacher-training college run by the Mercy nuns. The troupe was invited by Phyllis Wilson, Myles's wife, who ran a Bible study group for Carysfort students. When they tallied the numbers in the audience over a couple of days, it appeared that the entire student body had turned up! Phyllis ended up with 25% of the college in her study groups.

Myles and I remain slightly embarrassed that our management of their month-long tour did not quite match the bravado of the actors. But Irish Rail distinguished themselves when Jeff and company got to Galway and the woman in charge of the van to transport their scenery didn't show up. The stationmaster lent them a massive luggage cart (the Harbingers were convinced it was 'from the 19th century' – no doubt it was). It was then a matter of press-ganging every passing student,

121

new friend, or innocent passer-by, to push the scenery to UCG, starting with *uphill* through Eyre Square.

Later they told us about how they got to University College Cork. Sue got there first. She (plus toddler) had taken a late train, arriving at midnight. Exhausted, she went into the station loo and cried. An attentive member of the train staff heard her and asked what was wrong. Then the train engineer weighed in and took her to his home nearby where his wife put on a spread of tea and biscuits fit for a princess until Jeff, who had travelled from Dublin by a rickety old van, worked out where she was and rescued her.

We featured Cork again in another national tour, this time by Fr Franciszek Blachnicki, a survivor of the Auschwitz concentration camp in World War II. In 1942 he had been condemned to be beheaded by guillotine. By his own account, Blachnicki had a radical conversion to God, privately in his cell. Then the sentence was changed to ten years in prison '*after* the war'. The Americans liberated his camp before any sentence could be carried out. He decided to express his new devotion to God by becoming a priest and quickly found himself resisting the Polish communist regime, like he had resisted the Nazis. Our student friends from Ireland had gone to help 'Father B' when he began a 50,000-strong youth Bible movement across Poland. Now he came to Ireland to touch base.

In Blachnicki's lecture in Cork he claimed that young Polish people were being brave in the face of government repression, not due to traditional religion or nationalism, but 'due to the fact that in recent times the Polish people have begun to accept Jesus as their personal Lord'. Fr Seán McGann, the chaplain at University College Cork at the time, found this all a bit 'naïve' in the review he wrote for *The Fold* magazine. Considering Father B's personal experience of the situation, it was rather daring of Seán McGann to contradict him but he admitted that 'We would be very silly to ignore the genuine questions posed for the institutional church'[8] by groups such as the Agapé student group.

With such rickety beginnings did the Cork student group develop. But, in time, a student with leadership instinct arrived on the UCC scene from Charleville. He was Peadar Somers. He was the kind of leader who is prepared to stick his head above the ramparts, ably aided and abetted by Ray McNicholas from Agapé. Peadar decided to be the front man for a whole week of Christian exposure, simply called 'Christian Week'. Inside the space of seven days they managed to pack in a lecture on 'What Marx got right', the Irish première of an international film, a medical wizard, a debate with author Mary Kenny and, not one, but two ex-paramilitaries from the North.

The medic was Dr Denis Burkitt. A native of Enniskillen, County Fermanagh, he had spent 20 years as a surgeon in Africa. He addressed the medical faculty and also provided a lecture for the medically uninitiated like me. 'People often come to see me lecture because

---

8   The Fold, Cork Diocese, March 1984

they think I must surely be dead,' Dr Burkitt quipped, since he had already had a disease named after him (Burkitt's lymphoma). He had discovered this disease by doggedly correlating the symptoms from which his patients suffered when he worked in the highlands of Uganda.

Not only so, he then went on to be credited as 'the man who put fibre in our diet' since he realised that people who didn't eat much fibre tended to succumb more quickly to a range of diseases. The claim for which he was best remembered in his lectures was, 'When I see my friends from the highlands [where they had a fibre-rich diet] come down to the city, that's a warning sign. When a man starts carrying a briefcase, his health may be in danger!'

Dr Burkitt went on to say, 'To neglect spiritual food for your soul has a similar effect as the neglect of fibre in your diet has on your body. I am firmly convinced that we are spiritual beings in temporary biological bodies. Being clever is all right, but to be successful in this life and the next, you need the Lord as your guide and the Bible as your map.'

He gave no story, in his own experience, of a sudden turn-around to faith in Christ. Far from being any quick lurch, he said, 'The key was how I set my sail when I started at university.' He urged the new medical students to do likewise and then he burst forth into a poem by Ella Wheeler Wilcox:

One ship sails East,
And another West,
By the self-same winds that blow,
'Tis the set of the sails
And not the gales,

That tells the way we go.
Like the winds of the sea
Are the waves of time,
As we journey along through life,
'Tis the set of the soul,
That determines the goal,
And not the calm or the strife.[9]

Understandably, the general public expected the ex-paramilitaries to be the star turn of the week. They were Liam McCloskey, a hunger-striker who had previously been in the INLA (Irish National Liberation Army) and David Hamilton, previously a member of the UVF (Ulster Volunteer Force). Both men had served time in prison fairly recently, and both claimed, very believably, that their lives had been miraculously spared.

Both Liam and David credited Christ, not just for their rescue from participation in violent conflict but, more fundamentally, for God's forgiveness. The effect on how they now conducted their lives was dramatic. Even appearing on the same platform was a showstopper. They hadn't come to say that they had renounced their backgrounds and political philosophies (they hadn't).

---

9   World Voices, Ella Wheeler Wilcox, New York : Hearst's International Library Company, 1916.

It was simply that, once they had submitted to Christ, a higher Power had taken them over. They had eyesight to see things from their former enemies' point of view.

In Liam's case, he said it started with his cellmate, Kevin, who later died in the 1981 hunger strike. Kevin was in the habit of praying, so Liam tried it. 'The only thing to read in the cell was a Bible.' Liam made it all the way through to the words of Jesus in the Lord's Prayer, stopped at 'Forgive us our sins as we forgive those who sin against us,' and began to think through how that would ever work for him. How exactly would he go about forgiving those he had seen as enemies all these years? Then he began to think about the prayer of St. Francis of Assisi, 'Grant that I may not so much seek to be consoled as to console; to be understood, as to understand.' Again, he began to think, 'What if I had been born into a family in the other culture? How can I understand what it would mean to be brought up like one of my enemies?'

Then Kevin died, after just less than six weeks on the hunger strike. Liam took his place, an arrangement already made. 'After a few weeks I began to think about Jesus again – his fasting for forty days. Not long after my fortieth day on the hunger strike I began to lose my eyesight. It eventually packed up. Soon I was into the week when I was expecting to die – they knew how long it took. The next thing I knew the whole strike was called off during that same week.'

Now it was decision time – militancy or God? By this stage Liam was in hospital. His decision was communicated to God in a simple prayer and to the para-military organisation in a short letter of resignation. He was moved to a different prison, in Magilligan, where he not only prayed for his former enemies but could now pray *with* some of them. And he slowly regained his sight. This amazing mixture of people was held together by an organisation appropriately named 'Prison Fellowship'.

Next up on the UCC stage was one of those former enemies, David Hamilton. 'When I was a teenager, I went to a youth club in North Belfast. Some guys came in one Friday evening in combat fatigues carrying a stack of uniforms and laid them on the table-tennis table. They said, "We're starting a Protestant paramilitary group to fight the IRA. Hands up who wants to join?" That began a disaster period in my life.' Most chilling was his account of being confronted by a gunman who aimed at David's head at close range – but the weapon jammed and the man ran away in a panic.

The long arm of the law caught up with David. Lying in his prison cell one night his mind got fixated on the near scrapes he had had. He was convinced that God was after him, not to blame him but to forgive him. Just on the basis of the paper-thin information he had about Jesus, he decided to turn himself in for God's amnesty. David waited until his cellmate fell asleep and prayed that God would take him on. All the evidence says that God did. He woke up in the morning so happy that the cellmate noticed and ran out into the corridor to shout to everyone, 'Hallelujah! Packie's joined the God squad!'

'Packie' was David's prison nickname – everybody had one. His cellmate's was 'Bungalow' ('nothing upstairs').

Christian Week at UCC was also a family occasion for us. Our sons, Joel and Seán (ten and eight years old) accompanied us because they could meet a real live film star. The star was Brian Deacon and the film was Jesus, which played to a packed-out Irish première at the university on 1st November 1984. The film, depicting the life of Christ using the text of scripture, was directed by Peter Sykes and John Krish, and shot on location in 1979. From the beginning, the film was intended for an international audience and was released in various languages over the years that followed.

Brian Deacon, an English film and TV actor, who played the part of Jesus in the film, manfully did his duty on première night and answered questions from the public, including intrusive ones about his own spirituality. The next morning, he was on duty again in Jury's Hotel as he met with Joel and Seán (and yes, we did take photos of 'Joel and Seán with Jesus'). The boys were amazed because he looked so unlike the man in the film – until he told them that he had to wear a prosthetic nose in the film. He wore it for nine months, getting it fitted on and off every day!

Things have moved on since. The last time I checked, you could watch the Jesus Film on your smart phone in any one of 2,000 languages, including Irish. It now appears in the Guinness Book of Records as 'the world's most translated film'. But in Ireland they saw it first in the Rebel County and gave the proceeds of the première to GOAL, the humanitarian organisation, for the relief of famine in Ethiopia. By 2015 every Irish-speaking primary school (Gaelscoileanna), north and south, had a copy of the film.

Once you'd experienced the Rebel County was there anywhere else to go? Apparently there was, but it was far from Cork.

CHAPTER 12

PESHAWAR

The next year curiosity got the better of us, so Pam and I decided to go to Asia to see for ourselves what place there was for Irish people willing to reach across cultures with the story about Jesus. Georgia Coates, who was at that time in UCD, elected to go with us. We chose to research the viability of Irish personnel in Pakistan and even specified the Pathan people, who lived in Pakistan's North West Frontier Province, as a particular group that held our interest.

We took the regular route to travel – obligatory vaccinations, sick for two days, sore arms from injections, sore bottoms from gamma globulin shots, sore heads from wondering how Joel and Seán would be cared for in our absence. We needn't have worried about the boys – my parents flexed by coming to Dublin before we left and then bringing them to Strabane. We were still slightly anxious as we drove away from our home in Avondale Lawn in Blackrock – only to look in the car mirror and see the lads dancing for joy in the street like wild things, in their pyjamas.

We began learning about Eastern culture in Heathrow. The Pakistan International Airlines flight to Karachi was delayed because it had been decided to combine our flights with an earlier one. The man in charge of seating allocation seemed to be part of the cause of the delay as he couldn't peel the seat number labels off the chart. He had eaten his fingernails ('the girls are better at this') and was now reduced to laboriously prying off the labels with a bent staple. Once through the electronic surveillance machine, the mainly Pakistani passengers began to feel at home in the departure lounge. For us, this took a bit of getting used to because feeling at home meant for them that the men sat on the chairs and the women on the carpeted floor. I don't know what they thought of PIA's choice of in-flight movie – *Fame*.

By the time we landed in Rawalpindi the next morning I had worked out that it would be faster for us to deplane and take the short flight to Lahore, our ticketed destination. So Georgia, Pam and I got off and were bustled through passport control. I then spent ten minutes trying to understand the baggage carousels, of which there were two. One went round and round; the other went in a straight line, dumping bags in a pyramid only occasionally reduced by a foray of anxious passengers.

A sympathetic Pakistani businessman from London warned me that I would end up paying money for my re-routing and suggested we get right back on the plane we just got off. My insecurity had now reached a sufficient level that I took his advice and we proceeded to fly an additional 1,200 miles that day, courtesy of PIA. At least this allowed us to go through the transit desk in Karachi which was decorated with a poster bearing the words 'Hot tempers cause arguments, but patience brings peace. Proverbs, Chapter 15, Verse 18.' PIA's choice of music for landing in Lahore was Sibelius' *Finlandia.*

We wanted to meet people from Ireland who had an effective missionary work in Pakistan, and by eleven o'clock in the morning on Day One we visited Lahore's University of the Punjab and were introduced to a Trinity College Dublin graduate who was running private Bible studies for young Pakistani men interested in learning more about Christian faith. Over the next couple of days, we also interviewed various Pakistani Christians involved in Bible distribution and student outreach not unlike our own at home in Ireland.

One of them was Prof Daniel Bakhsh, a cheery psychologist, who introduced us to his family and friends in their home. At the end of our visit somebody suggested that we sing something together that we, from our various cultures, would know. To my amazement we found a song which appears in both Urdu and English! It was *I have decided to follow Jesus* written by Sadhu Sundar Singh, a Sikh who had met ascetic holy men as a child. He then decided to also become an ascetic promoter for Christ all around South Asia after his teenage conversion. The tune is noticeably Eastern but has adapted, like traditional folk singing, to the Irish ear

– unexpected fusion music!

Also on day one we had a simple domestic wrinkle to iron out. The person at St Hilda's hostel, where we were staying, had reckoned on 'Georgia Coates' being a baby girl so they kindly provided a small cot in the room which had been assigned to Pam and me. A single woman floating around on her own sounded to them like a tropical bird, so they worked out that this booking must be for a child of ours. The issue was quickly corrected with some embarrassment on their part and a lot of apologising, but this was a lesson which came in handy when we booked places to stay on our onward itinerary.

The Pathan people lived in a district nearly 200 miles north-west of Lahore so we flew to the city of Peshawar, the provincial capital. My seat companion on the flight was a dapper Pathan in his late twenties. 'Do you often fly on this route?' I asked. 'Usually,' he said pleasantly. I tried to sort that one out. Did he mean that when the plane flew he usually went with it? That's what he seemed to mean at face value so I asked him what he did for a living. 'I am a star,' he said. Well, that was one thing clear. But I proceeded to ask, 'What kind of star?' 'A television and film star,' said my companion, 'I'm probably in the paper today, come to think of it.'

There followed much unfastening and fastening of seat belts as we reached into an empty forward seat for a daily newspaper. There he was on the TV listings page, Firdous Jamal, the star of some turgid on-going drama which was apparently compulsive viewing. He shared his successes in life (film roles mainly) and his aspiration which was to play Shakespeare in England. 'And what about you, what do you do?' he asked. 'I am a devotee of Jesus of Nazareth and I teach about him, especially to young people,' I said.

The star obviously held Jesus in high regard since he began to share the personal struggles of his life. I explained that his struggles were something that Jesus had dealt with, and dealt with well. We talked about this all the way through the airport terminal after landing. We exchanged addresses and I left him with a copy of a letter that a friend of mine had written to someone experiencing the same life struggles.

We were met by local friends with whom we had corresponded, who were involved in refugee relief work. They brought us to Jan's hotel. They said, 'There are two hotels, Dean's and Jan's. Dean's has the journalists.' I think that was meant to explain why we weren't going there.

To get acclimatised to our surroundings we bought local clothes because we really didn't want to stand out in the crowd. Appropriately decked out in shalwar kameez, we checked out some bookshops. In the first shop we were slowly browsing along the shelves, came to the end of a row and someone's head popped around the corner of the aisle with a slow laconic, 'How'rya', in a distinctly Cavan accent. Not exactly what we had expected.

She was Barbara Geddes, whom we had once met briefly in Dublin and was now working with a refugee relief service called SERVE. Barbara had served with distinction to advance the welfare of Pathans with the United Nations in Jalalabad and now in Peshawar. Barbara's unshakeable personality and deadpan turn of phrase seemed a natural choice for the relief agency. Her services were especially welcome because, being Irish, she did not need a visa, whereas relief workers of other nationalities spent a lot of their time to-ing and fro-ing to get residence permits.

The influx of refugee Pathans from Afghanistan gave the North West Frontier Province one of the largest refugee populations in the world. The SERVE people showed us around their scheme, which taught carpet-weaving to orphaned boys so they could begin to support themselves. This seemed to me to make sense as it gave these teenagers power over their own destiny. At the end of the training period each boy was given a loom and enough wool to weave his first carpet on his own. That way he would not have to live beholden to the big-time carpet operators who often owned the village looms.

One of the carpet boys had relatives living in the refugee camp just out of town and we arranged to go out to visit them, with a translator. How they found the tent amidst a refugee camp housing half a million people I do not know. We were treated with great cordiality and soon found that Pathans were no ordinary refugees. They preserved tremendous dignity and looked us in the eye as equals. The men sat in the tent with us. The women made fresh bread (naan) and chai (which was boiled for

20 minutes with the sugar and milk).

They had been there two years. Apparently they had all gone back to fight in Afghanistan during that time. The orphan's father had been brave. Some of those present would return to the fight in four days. Their commander had just been featured in *Le Figaro* newspaper. 'We would have won long ago if it weren't for the Russian helicopter gunships. All we need now is surface-to air-missiles,' they said.

They were quite insistent on this business of the surface-to-air missiles, pressing the issue on me, as if I could do anything about it, which spooked me. Our friends from SERVE said, 'They're talking to you like that just because you're a Western visitor and they hope one day some Western visitor will appear with money or political connections.' Little did we realise that shortly after we left, a US Congressmen called Charlie Wilson slipped into town – with the money and the political connections. (Surface-to-air missiles appeared as if by magic. In a surreal twist Pam and I were able to see all this portrayed over twenty years later in the film *Charlie Wilson's War*, with Charlie played by Tom Hanks. That *really* spooked me.)

Barbara gave us a special treat one day by bringing us to visit the local Presentation nuns, most of whom were from Cavan too and universally respected in the city. From the inside there was little to indicate that this convent wasn't in Fermoy, Athlone or Clonmel. We had tea (with adroitly reconstituted Irish powdered milk) and talked for an hour and a half with Sister Monica who had worked in Peshawar for 45 years. Surely one of the 'grand old ladies' of Irish missions, she spoke with verve and enthusiasm about her 'pre-evangelization' work in the local school and commented hopefully and without batting an eyelid, 'I expect these people to turn back to Christianity in two hundred years.' It was refreshing to meet someone with such a sense of history who sees herself as a person of destiny and who could work with contentment towards a goal beyond her own lifetime – in her case 2181 AD. I don't know many people who even think like that.

The other major educational institution we visited was the red-brick University of Peshawar with over 8,000 students, all residential. On this visit I was joined by Jim, a SERVE specialist in integrated development who had had a one-sided correspondence with the Deputy Registrar who was now, in person, ever so apologetic for not answering, 'I rarely answer on account of the price and my overworking.' I went to see Dr Anwar of the Central Asia Study Centre to ask if I could study Pathan culture and language there. He was very encouraging. I think he was pleased that somebody wanted to learn his language – who wouldn't be? I was surprised that the university's handbook even advertised a student loan scheme – way ahead of its time. It took us a good part of the afternoon to visit the departments we wanted to see, and appointments were often delayed (maybe because of more 'overworking').

On one of these long breaks between appointments I took the opportunity to wander slowly around the sparse lawn in front of the building. After a while I noticed a man waving at me. He was in the shadow of a tree so I couldn't make him out clearly. More waving followed and eventually he came into the sunlight. To my chagrin I now noticed the massive tribal turban on his head and the rifle hanging from his shoulder. This concentrated my mind. He got nearer, speaking quietly. I stood my ground and sweated. As he came to my personal space he gave up talking and reverted to sign language, which he was good at. He had taken pity on me standing out there in the hot sun and wanted me to enjoy the shade of the trees before I keeled over with dehydration. He was a security guy for the university. The intricately patterned turban was a normal, distinctive, proud tribal sign – like a surname.

Suitably chastened, it was now my turn to see Dr Sattar, head of chemistry, who told me that they taught 'some elementary microbiology' – my old speciality from Trinity College. I offered to teach it (the blood must have gone to my head). 'How many hours a week?' he asked. (The blood must have gone to his head too.)

Jim invited me to join him on a visit to Islamabad to try to sort out his visa. We took the journey on the GTS bus (Government Transport Service) which hurtled through the sleeping pre-dawn countryside in two hours and fifty minutes. By noon we had trekked through half a dozen government offices and ended up in the ministry of Rural Development to talk to the Joint Secretary. The Secretary's secretary had told us to expect him in after lunch. Lunchtime came and went without an appearance. By this time the sun, lack of food and dehydration was getting to me and my body said, 'Time to go to sleep.'

So there was nothing for it but to lie down on the Joint Secretary's sofa, while Jim sat vigil over me. Nobody seemed to be bothered by this – apparently I wasn't the first – and quite a bit of traffic continued to go through the office, but never the Joint Secretary. When I awoke, we repaired to the Holiday Inn about half a mile away where we made phone calls, used the bathroom, watched an Arab sheikh, listened to rock music, changed money, ate and, most of all, drank. Over a cool glass of safe water, I told Jim, 'You know friend, things would be much easier if you could just be Irish.'

It took another visit to Islamabad to get definitive word on the visa and again I went with Jim. We were kindly hosted by Jim's friend, Latif Bhatti, where we shared a room. No sooner had we retired for the night, when the heavens opened and we were treated to voluminous rain, hailstones, thunder and lightning – and people walking through our room to get a better view of all this from our window. Jim thought that was a bit odd. So did I. We reckoned there must be a whole lot more to learn about local culture. The next day we decided that since we had to wait for various government departments to move we could profitably spend the time visiting Murree Christian School.

This amazing school provided an international education for children of missionaries in Asia. We took the two-hour wagon transport which navigated a never-ending series of corkscrew bends. The school was built on the outskirts of the town of Murree, perched on the mountain with a grandstand view of the foothills of the Himalayas. The principal, Mr Roub, showed us around and we chatted with kids from Germany, Korea, the USA and the UK. Another two hours of careering down the mountain returned us from Murree's quaint, rickety, hillside town, built, layer upon layer, over a century, to Islamabad – the ultimate capital city, designed on a grid, scarcely twenty years old.

Before we left Peshawar we still had another few items to attend to. One was to get the tourist experience of the Khyber Pass. On Easter Sunday, no less, a group of us hired a taxi which roared up that iconic road to the border with Afghanistan, with its border post of Russian-trained Afghan soldiers. The driver had enough well-practised English to show us the various spots in the Pass where one or another British regiment was wiped out by Pathan fighters during the nineteenth century Anglo-Afghan wars. Pathan respect for the British army remained high. I think they respected them for trying. The driver kept the car radio on. On the way back down it was playing the Beatles' *Hey Jude*.

Perhaps the most courteous person I had the pleasure of interviewing in Peshawar was Norman Green, the principal of Edwardes College which was founded by missionaries in 1900 and is a constituent part of the University. Rev Green (he was an ordained Anglican with a degree in law) was the latest in a long line of British principals who had been installed since the beginning. He said he was 'totally disillusioned with classical missions' and I think that the idea of people like Pam and me settling there was his worst nightmare. I asked him if he thought Irish personnel could be effective. Just as if I had pushed a button there came out a bombardment of reasons why it wouldn't work. He was sure that we would never survive financially, couldn't get jobs or educate our children.

'Just look at the tide of Christianity in Pakistan,' he boomed, 'Is it coming in or going out? Anybody can see it's running out.' Norman's intense feeling may have been influenced by the fact that his forty-year tenure was itself coming to an end. The morning was sliding away so eventually I said, 'Well, I really must be going along,' stood up and he shook my hand. My journal records how we ended the conversation:

'At the end of 1½ hours of quick-fire non-stop discouragement he said, "If you carry the banner of Saint Paul, and have fire in your belly, nothing will stop you." And then after a whimsical moment's reflection "– not even me." '

My journal also shows how keen we still were to make some distance in our moving plans. I recorded that we went to see the Pakistan Air Force secondary school. This had been recommended to us for our children by a happy missionary who had sent his kids there. We had met his young teenage son who was tri-lingual in English, Urdu and Pakistani English, switching effortlessly between one and another, in company, depending on who was talking to him.

First we met the school's head teacher. She gave us the list of fees but said that we would need to talk to the man in charge who was an Air Force officer. When we were later ushered into the presence of Wing-Commander Pir Akram it was amidst a roomful of other military figures. He was most gracious and welcomed the prospect of our boys attending the school. 'They will teach our children too – and vice versa,' he predicted. As soon as I could, I met with the school's registrar, Miss Karshid Aziz, and filled out application forms for Joel and Seán to put them on the waiting list. For years thereafter when our son Joel introduced himself he remembered to include 'and I am registered for the Pakistan Air Force secondary school'!

The most detailed part of our plan was costing domestic appliances (the locals assured us that a room-cooler was a quarter the price of air-conditioning). And before we finally left town we also managed to fit in some introductory lessons in the Pashto language which was still ringing in our heads as PIA efficiently smoothed our way through three airports in Pakistan, one in Frankfurt and one in Heathrow. We immediately booked on to the Belfast Shuttle flight, landed at Aldergrove airport and were mad enough to drive straight to 31 Melmount Gardens in Strabane to meet our children. It was midnight. It felt like we had time-warped from another galaxy in one day.

A skewed sense of timing must rank as one of the biggest sources of mistakes in my life. We were ready to go to Peshawar, some people there would have cordially received us, even the Air Force school was looking forward to our children, *but* our Irish team members weren't ready to send us. We deferred to them. I thought maybe they could see issues that we couldn't see because my judgement was clouded by a sense of exotic adventure. Maybe they intuitively felt we had unfinished business in Ireland. As it turned out, they were right. We had another adventure about to begin, right there on our home turf.

CHAPTER 13

THE BISHOP AND THE
JOURNALIST

The first I knew about the 'Ballaghaderreen issue' was when somebody said, 'I see you're in the papers today.' It was 7th October 1981 and it wasn't *me* in the newspapers but, when somebody says that, your mind goes into overdrive. The *Irish Independent* was running an article entitled 'Bible Group quits Church' and it was about our Campus Crusade for Christ student group. The *Irish Press* had 'Bishop's plea to breakaway Catholics'. The next day there followed 'Bishop kept spy in breakaway group' in the *Press* and 'UCD and Trinity deny any "secret" campus cult' in the *Independent*. The next week saw a dozen articles in the national dailies, only one of which (by Patrick Nolan of the *Irish Times*) phoned us up to check the details. It cost us a fortune buying the newspapers every morning for a good while, always feeling like we were behind the wave, never ahead of it.

It didn't take long to find out where this story was coming from. Bishop Thomas Flynn of Achonry (in

Ballaghaderreen, County Roscommon), had recently written a pastoral letter 'Parents Wonder and Children Wander' which had somehow arrived on the papers' news-desks at the same time. Somebody sent me a copy.

His missive claimed that

'Campus Crusade are having the greatest influence in the Ballaghaderreen area...

'By virtue of their programme they have, in fact, made strong attacks on the Church...

'They go on from there to attack the Mass and all the sacraments. At University College Galway, they have uprooted a number of Catholics from their religion. The Galway group has gone further to ensure that some of their members have got teaching posts in Catholic Secondary Schools...

'Their attitude is Christ – yes: Church – NO'

Then a title, in capitals, introduced the main two-thirds of the document: 'THE BIBLE IS A DIFFICULT BOOK TO READ AND VERY FEW ARE COMPETENT TO UNDERSTAND IT WITHOUT HELP AND GUIDANCE.'[10]

There followed an earnest review of the fruit of the last hundred years' worth of Biblical research. It sounded to me like the bishop was doing his best to catch up his congregation on the latest in Scripture study (it included references to Plato and Virgil). By being so complicated he might have inadvertently been ever-so-slightly off-putting. But he finished the letter to his flock with a

---

10 Parents Wonder and Children Wander, Bishop Thomas Flynn, July 1981

worthy attitude to teenagers, with which no-one would disagree:

'Perhaps our adult world is talking at them too much and not listening enough to what they have to say. Do we give them everything they want except the time which they need so much? I ask myself if the Church has enough time for them either. And what about Hope? Do they see us trying to build a better world where concern and care for one another makes life worthwhile, and where fear and tension give way to hope and trust? Our Catholic world is not dead, but it may not be quite fully awake.'

I was quite perplexed as to how to respond. If I wrote to the bishop, I would need to match his exactitude. If I wrote to the papers, I would need to offer them something new to think about. I chose to write to the bishop first (and I copied it to the Cardinal, Tomás Ó Fiaich):

'Your pastoral letter "Parents Wonder and Children Wander" has recently come to hand and I feel it merits a responsible response. It appears from your letter that some confusion may have arisen between our work and that of the renewal group in Ballaghaderreen. We know some of those in this group as we made friends in the earliest days of the renewal in the West, and we continue to be personal friends.'

I then listed the things we had done to try to foster and bolster Christian faith amongst university students and graduates (which had included a fair bit of Biblical studies). Since the Sunday Independent had by now reported that the group included a self-confessed member of the Provisional IRA, I finished the letter by remarking that 'I am sure you will join with us in thanking God for the way in which the lifestyle of some of the Ballaghaderreen folk has radically changed for the better. Here is something we can surely all agree on. I would appreciate the opportunity of discussing these issues with you personally.'

The ever-vigilant bishop answered quite quickly, in his typical precise style. He wasn't ready to accept that some Ballaghaderreen lifestyles had been radically changed. Rather, he listed what he saw as their misdeeds, concluding with 'I honestly do not know what they possess as "virtues". To ignore a large part of the teaching of Christ is not a "virtue" as far as I am concerned. With kind regards, Sincerely yours, +Thomas Flynn, Bishop of Achonry''.

End of story. There was no talk of accepting my invitation for us to meet. Alas, that was not to be. However, as I was later to learn, we had not run out of bishops. There were others who were casting a wary eye on the scene with more benevolent attitudes, albeit silent for the moment. For a while we felt like our life was regulated by the scheduling of the regular Irish bishops' conference in Maynooth. If we were on their agenda, journalists would be snapping at their heels for a scrap of opinion as soon as business was over for the day. We were comforted by a couple of 'tame' bishops, Joe Cassidy and Brendan Comiskey, who did us the kind service of letting us know by lunchtime whether we were featured on the agenda. On occasion I would sneak out to meet them in a pub in Maynooth during the episcopal lunch break and get the low-down on whether their meeting was ploughing through the items too slowly to get down as far as us.

The newspaper barrage came to a head with an article by Joe Power in the *Evening Herald*, 'Church reacts to 'threat' of new cults'. It was obvious he was seeing how far he could get by innuendo. His claim was that we had 'capitalised on the apathy towards religion by young Irish boys and girls, and have used their impressive powers of persuasion to encourage others who are searching for the truth away from family-based religions, according to a Catholic Church spokesman.'

This time I jumped into action by delivering a letter by hand to their office:

'Last night I read with shock your article in the *Evening Herald* "Church reacts to 'threat' of new cults". Clarification is necessary and I hope that the following will help…

'We have no axe to grind as to which church people go to. In the various churches the concept of a "personal commitment to Christ" has become much more common of recent years. In some districts it appears that those who lobby for such a call to commitment are regarded as out of step and reactionary pressures try to stifle such voices by sticking the label of "cult" on them…

'When I contacted the Catholic Press and Information

office yesterday afternoon, they were not aware of your article…Fr John Wilson, of the Archbishop's office, told me last evening, "Your problem is with the newspaper. The Archbishop has issued no statement on this subject"…

'As for "family-based religion" – I am a family man myself. My parents, brother and sister are some of my closest friends. I have a wife and two sons who go to a national school where some of the teachers probably read the *Evening Herald*. Go easy on them. At this point the only course open to us which would redress the balance is for me to submit an article, which I am sending over this morning. Please ask your editor to give it his urgent attention, by which I mean – if it stands up on its own merits, print it this week. Thank you. Yours sincerely, David Wilson.'

The *Herald* extracted my letter down to a few sentences and printed it in 'Letters to the Editor' under the title 'No Sects Please'. At least their sub-editors were awake! Still quite hot and bothered, I wrote in high dudgeon to a member of our Board, Miss Margaret Hamilton Reid, who was also on the Board of Switzers department store, to ask her to do something – anything. She replied, 'I do not take the *Evening Herald*.' That calmed me down. There's more to life. One of our kind sponsors reassured us, 'Don't worry. You know what will kill today's headlines? – tomorrow's headlines.'

I was called upon, by the Debating Society at University College Galway, to engage the Bishop of

Galway, Eamon Casey, in a debate on 'Being born again' (I was for it, the bishop was against it). This also put me in a curious position because the BBC in Belfast thought this would be a suitable topic for their radio programme 'Sunday Sequence'. I went in to the RTE studio in Dublin for an interview 'down the line' from Belfast, only to find that my interviewer was a guy called Trevor Williams whom I had known since childhood. He held it together (as did I!) and pretended we were talking for the first time and he put his penetrating questions to me with as much objectivity as he could muster (which wasn't much).

Back in Ballaghaderreen, Bishop Flynn still had homework to do. A teacher in the local prayer group in the town wrote to us recalling that she had graduated from Galway University two years previously:

'I majored in Psychology and Communications in my search for authentic relationships (which I now know was a search for God)...

I saw that faith was not a blind leap in the dark but a moving ahead in faith based on the facts of God's Word. Discovering this was an answer to my deepest desires as it led me to discover a life worth sharing with others...

One of my desires is to counsel others, and as a teacher I often have opportunities to do this. I now know that the greatest help I can give is to be able to lead them to Christ.'

It had started as a trickle of graduates going back home to take up local jobs, radicalised with a vision of changing the world through the love of Christ. This then led to a trickle of priests coming down to Galway to find out what had changed those students' perspective. It looked like some students were more developed in their spiritual thinking than those who were professionally employed to do their thinking for them.

One priest from Mayo told us he had been assigned to the island of Inis Mór (in the Aran Islands). 'I'm going to Aran. I'm going to get myself a rock and a Bible and I'm going to sit on that rock and read the Bible for three years.' That kind of determination is what led to a movement in the western counties that would take more than a bishop to stop.

And we learned about newspapers. My brother Myles met his neighbour Conor Brady, then editor of the *Irish Times*, at a Christmas party. Conor said, 'You're having a hard time of it in the papers. Do you send out press releases?' 'We have no time left for that kind of thing,' Myles replied, 'we're too busy putting out fires.' 'Give it a go,' suggested Conor, 'Don't expect them to print your piece but they will file it. Some day in the future they will need to write about you and, because they're lazy, they will use the copy you sent them. The question is when that day comes, do you want them to use your words or their words?'

That was the week we began to send out press releases, which then became a monthly habit. We shared our news, in printed press releases, about all kinds of people and events which may have looked a bit boring.

But we never had any further trouble from the print media about bishops and cults. They even published our own stories from time to time.

In one way I was like Bishop Flynn – I wouldn't budge. In my case the principle on which I wouldn't budge was that we weren't going to endorse any particular denomination for our new Jesus-following graduate friends. Their new free life included the freedom to make up their own minds. Some of them resented this a bit – they thought we could at least make recommendations. I wasn't moving. Maybe it was the simplicity of my 'Gospel Hall' background kicking in.

But the next time I heard of a Gospel Hall was in a context that nobody ever wants to experience.

CHAPTER 14

A PRIMER IN
FORGIVING

I was driving out to Dublin airport to pick up an old friend on the evening of Sunday, November 20th 1983, when I idly flicked on the car radio to listen to the eight o'clock news. Little did I realize that what I was about to hear would radically change my timetable for a couple of weeks and would utterly change the lives of others.

The news reported that gunmen had rushed into a 'Gospel Hall' in the border area and had shot three men dead during a worship service. My blood ran cold since I was brought up in a Gospel Hall in County Tyrone half a mile from the border. I stared ahead as I drove out the Santry bypass, scarcely able to believe what I had just heard. The reports were still skimpy at that stage since the shooting had happened (in Darkley, County Armagh) only a couple of hours earlier. The church was actually called the Mountain Lodge Pentecostal Assembly.

Something had turned deep within me because of the mention (mistakenly as it happens) of a 'Gospel Hall'.

I had the oddest desire to forget my friend at the airport and just keep on driving. It was like a homing instinct. They, whoever 'they' were, had got some of 'our' people.

You see, in the Gospel Halls where I was brought up, politics was avoided like the plague. We were brought up to believe that anyone who had chosen identification with Jesus was, *de facto*, a 'citizen of heaven'. Few in our church even felt obliged to vote in general elections. So I thought that the day would never come when we would be attacked on political grounds. Politics has passed us by – or rather – *we* had passed *it* by. Later theories about Darkley proposed that it was just such political naivety that singled out the church for attack – so that their very innocence would provoke widespread civil unrest.

For the first time I was feeling the feeling that has gripped so many over the years – 'they got one of ours'. This time 'they', whoever they were, had attacked the politically naive.

I did stop at the airport, played my friend the nine o'clock news on the radio, drove home and listened to every bulletin until I went to bed at midnight. The midnight bulletin had more detail on the church – it was in a loose association of independent churches. I went to sleep fitfully, with a sinking feeling that no end of praying seemed to cure.

I woke the next morning to find that RTE had produced a priest (Fr Billy Fitzgerald) to give a special message for the day at 7:25 a.m. Fr Billy manfully faced the gruesome news and spoke in subdued tones of the possibility of forgiveness in the midst of such courage. 'Good morning,' he began, 'if I really can call it a good morning.' It was a courageous thing to do, to try to bring hope into an apparently hopeless situation.

I asked friends to pray for me that God would control my 'tribal' feelings and that I could find some way to respond to the situation. There wasn't much that could be done but I wanted to do something. I phoned an old friend of mine, Paddy Monaghan, an influential Catholic layman. It was agreed, as soon as funeral arrangements had been made, that a delegation from Dublin would attend the funerals, representing believers from all walks of life. This was something I *could* participate in by way of response.

One of the unnerving things for me about the shooting was that one of those killed was also called David Wilson. On that first day after the massacre his sister pled for no reprisals. As *The Irish Times* reported, 'Speaking at the family farm outside Keady she said: "Let there be no tit-for-tat killings. In God's name let there be no reprisals." '[11]

On Tuesday, before the funeral of Victor Cunningham (one of the elders who was shot), Cardinal O'Fiaich and other church leaders visited his widow, Edna. After the visit, the Cardinal said that he had been 'most impressed by Mrs Cunningham's courage, resignation and readiness to forgive her husband's killers'. Describing her as a 'person of great faith' he made the point that

---

11 Irish Times, November 22, 1983

'the first word on her lips was forgiveness'.[12] Amongst the thousands who attended the funerals of the other two men the next afternoon was the inter-church delegation from Dublin.

We drove past the church building which now looked so vulnerable with the bullet holes in the walls marked with white circles by the police. Every road and laneway within a mile of the victims' homes was lined with cars so we walked that last mile – along with the hundreds who had similarly come in sympathy and solidarity. We were expecting a non-political funeral and, true to form, they did not disappoint us. Even on the hearse that carried another elder, Harold Brown, I noticed two wreaths, side by side. One was from prison officers and the other from the 'Soldiers of the Cross', a movement of ex-paramilitaries now committed to Christ.

At the graveside the pastor of Mountain Lodge, Bob Bain, had the last word. He said he was like the captain of the ship who was asked in the midst of a storm what he was going to do. His reply: 'Whether the ship goes up or down, we're going on!' Then he told mourners why he was confident that God could forgive those who had committed the murders. His rationale was simple: 'After all, God has forgiven us. So why *wouldn't* he forgive anyone else who repents.'

In the context of so many Northern Ireland funeral messages of recrimination and condemnation, Pastor Bain's approach was stunningly refreshing. His spirit of

---

12 Irish Times, November 23, 1983

perseverance was then displayed when he announced that we were now going to finish the singing of the hymn that had been interrupted when the congregation had been fired on three days earlier. I could hardly believe that the hundreds of mourners thronging the graveyard were going to suck up their emotions and successfully accomplish this feat – but we did.

By the time I got back into the car in Newry the hymn was still ringing in my ears:

'Have you been to Jesus for the cleansing power?

Are you washed in the blood of the Lamb?

Are you fully trusting in His grace this hour?

Are you washed in the blood of the Lamb?' [13]

Again the news broadcasts carried the story about forgiveness, *and* the hymn. When I heard the hymn on the car radio I laughed. It was a laugh I hadn't expected that came from somewhere in my stomach and jumped out of my mouth. I was laughing that Satan had over-stepped himself. His attempt to disturb God's people had backfired seriously as the news of being forgiven by Jesus was now spreading across the country and in the next few hours across the world. At the six o'clock news the same thing happened. I hadn't had a good laugh for days.

The following Sunday, Darkley was in the news once more as RTE let the people in Mountain Lodge Pentecostal Assembly speak for themselves, and one of their elders, Jimmy Burney, again said, 'We pray for the

---

13 Elisha Albright Hoffman, Spiritual Songs for Gospel Meetings and the Sunday School. Cleveland, Ohio: Barker & Smellie, 1878.

men who did this. We will be glad to have them come back to our church. We will pray that God will forgive them.'

It was two months before Darkley appeared in the news again and this time it was another front page splash in the Dublin papers – for their church re-opening. The *Irish Press* newspaper reported that:

'Pastor Bain reflected the spirit of forgiveness that was evident less than twenty-four hours after the attack when he said: "There is repentance for these men if they come and repent at the foot of the Cross. God will forgive them. I feel in my heart that if they came in here in repentance I would be the first man to pray for them," he declared.'[14]

In an *Irish Times* article entitled 'Darkley church still prays for the sinners,' Fionnuala O'Connor continued the saga by reporting how the pastor was quoting the lines of yet another hymn:

' "I stand amazed in the presence of Jesus," said Pastor Bain, pacing up and down, his coat off, his sleeves rolled up. "I wonder how He could love me, a sinner. What about you? Are you outside on such a day of uncertainty? Just mind our brothers taking off so suddenly. Now they are praising Him up there. They've met the Saviour. If they had not been saved they would have been lost." '[15]

Sometimes I wonder if this kind of report makes any difference at all to the person in the street. I'm beginning

---

14 Irish Press, January 23, 1984

15 Irish Times, January 23. 1984

to think it does. A few weeks later I took a taxi from home to Heuston Station very early one morning to catch the Cork train. The taxi driver asked if my trip was business or pleasure. I was actually going to give a day-long seminar at U.C.C. on Bible study so I told him it was business all right but pleasant business, explaining what lay ahead in the plan for the day.

'But do you believe all that stuff in the Bible?' he said, 'Half of it's not even practical.' 'What do you mean?' I asked. 'Well, take the Sermon on the Mount. All that stuff about turning the other cheek and forgiving your enemies. Sure nobody really does that nowadays. It's not practical.'

I said that I thought that it was practical if you were prepared to also take on board the power that Jesus offered to implement his teaching. 'I think I can prove it to you,' I suggested. 'What about the people in Darkley?'

'Ah, but that's different,' said the taxi driver. 'There's a big difference between them and me. If you looked into it, I bet you'd find that every last man Jack in that place is a believer. That's why it works for them.' He never spoke a truer word.

My brother Myles and his wife Phyllis soon provided us with a close-up lens on Northern life. They moved from Dublin to work in Belfast on designing a communication medium which would explain how allegiance to Jesus works out. Considering that the North seemed locked into a historic cocktail of church, politics and culture, that was an unenviable task. Most Northerners thought they knew enough about Jesus and, what's more, they belonged to a church which specialised in this sort of thing. Was there any way to penetrate through this level of fog?

In 2021 I went to see Myles and Phyllis to get the story straight. We met for lunch in the Hilton Hotel, helpfully located beside the station where the train arrives from Dublin. First I asked Myles about the magazine, entitled *There is Hope*, which he had famously worked on at that time. 'Was that your solution to the Northern situation?' 'Not at all,' he said, 'that was just a visible part of it. The best way to describe what we did is this: we made a noise.

'The whole thing began when I was back in Strabane one day and looked down on the town from a hilly road and watched a man casually walking up the street. I asked myself, "How is that man ever, *ever*, going to understand the plain gospel of Jesus?"

'So I invited the churches to use their 1986 Lent and Easter season to promote the message "There is Hope". I pulled a small team together [nobody like Myles if you're ever looking for a puller-together]. Hope was rare in those days. In fact, we contacted every single Protestant and Catholic church in the North four times before the "There is Hope" campaign started. We promised to help them by providing printed banners, a magazine, national publicity. Over three hundred of them, of all shades, took up the offer. Hope was just the thing many churches were wanting to talk about in the midst of the tribal strife of the time.'

So far, so good. They were getting buy-in from progressive thinkers. Churches got busy hanging enormous 'There is Hope' banners with a rainbow logo outside their buildings (some left them hanging there for a further two years). Myles, meanwhile, got busy on a family magazine which was enticing enough to pull in readers of all ages. It didn't bother him that he'd never published a magazine before. All he needed was a couple of dozen articles, competent writers, an experienced editor, pictures, a printer, copyright permissions, advertisers, distributors – and, oh yes, sponsors. He scoured the countryside looking for enthusiasts for whom allegiance to Jesus trumped their particular denominational background.

What Myles and Phyllis *didn't* expect to get was death threats. 'We got warning calls from the police and "Out, out, out" daubed on the wall of our house,' they tell me. They were doing too much reconciliation for some people's liking. One church that led the way in reconciliation (Fitzroy Presbyterian in Belfast) invited the Catholic bishop (Cathal Daly) and the moderator of the Presbyterian church (Dr Robert Dickenson) to speak on 'There is Hope in Christ'. On paper it sounded like a serene Tuesday evening. In reality the 600 people who turned up were treated to an hour of heckling and fisticuffs by intruders who were only held in check by a significant police presence.

Myles's resolve was only strengthened. The magazine ended up in every one of the 600,000 homes in Northern

Ireland (plus or minus a few Post Office goofs). Somehow a copy got into a prison and helped a prisoner experience a life turn-around as he read about a whole new world of normality he hadn't experienced. The articles covered everything from football to fitness to communication in marriage, quizzes – and, of course, an article entitled, tellingly, 'Jesus, the man you thought you knew', with a list of cinemas all across the North which were showing the *Jesus Film*. To the surprise of the Curzon cinema in Belfast, 6,000 people turned up to see the film, out-selling *Out of Africa*.

Myles's team pulled all the strings they knew and secured an interview with Norman Whiteside, the Belfast boy who had signed for Manchester United at the age of 17 and went on to be the youngest player ever to take part in a FIFA World Cup. The cook, Delia Smith, popped up with a recipe. There were real-life accounts of triumph and tragedy, features on U2 and the 1970 Eurovision Song Contest winner, Dana. In fact, Dana let her picture be used on the magazine's cover and gave tips on how to rear your children and pray with them.

Dana also agreed to sing at an event to support 'There is Hope'. At the last minute the man who had signed the insurance for the event telephoned Myles to say the event 'couldn't possibly go ahead' because he 'couldn't possibly take responsibility for insuring a big-name event'. He obviously hadn't realised he was dealing with someone with a steel backbone like Myles, who said, 'Well, you signed it.'

But Myles isn't merciless. When the insurance agent pleaded, 'OK, let me check with the underwriter,' Myles agreed and said, 'Fine, you do that and I'll check with you every so often to see how you're getting on.' Much relieved, Mr Insurer took a note to check on the terms and conditions as time permitted. Twenty minutes later Myles phoned him, sounding like the heart and soul of kind understanding, and asked how the 'checking' was coming along. The flustered agent had to blurt out, 'Not yet. Give me a little time.' Myles happily agreed and gave him a little time. After another half an hour he made another chirpy call. The half-hourly calls secured the insurance by lunchtime. Maybe the agent didn't notice that behind big-name Dana was the patient Myles and behind him was 'the man you thought you knew'.

Two other names appeared in the *There is Hope* magazine – Packie Hamilton and Liam McCloskey, the ex-paramilitaries who had made such an impression at University College Cork. Just even having them appear together in a photograph shouted, 'There *is* hope'. That vision of potential healing in society is a notion that Myles tucked away in his heart. He had already become known as the 'Rainbow Man' and it wasn't too long before he became a spokesperson for that vision on a much wider canvas.

For our family, brought up at that time in County Tyrone, Myles included, it was as plain as the nose on your face that understanding between the nationalist and unionist clans wasn't likely to break out unless there were ways to meet each other. Almost any way would do – playing football, going to the same school, playing in the same band. It still bewilders us that there was no obvious vehicle for the clans to meet. It would need some people to break taboos.

In 1991 Myles grasped a chance to do just that. He was contacted by Rev Trevor Morrow, Presbyterian minister in Lucan, County Dublin, to see if they could find a way to allow Northern Protestant and Catholic kids to do more than just play football together – not in Belfast, but in the Dublin area. They would need a safe space where they could come and unwind. Trevor felt passionately that this was almost their *duty* to provide a literal 'level playing field' for Northern kids to use, not so much for football but for spending time together, for knowing about each other. After all, each of them was made in God's image. He wanted Myles to chip in with some of his skills to make this embryonic idea become a reality. Myles agreed.

The Northern Ireland government had just launched a programme called 'Education for Mutual Understanding', a cross-cultural curriculum for all state-funded schools. It was about 'self respect and respect for others, and the improvement of relationships between people of differing cultural traditions'. Schools were only mildly enthusiastic about it because few knew how to do it. Trevor convinced the key people in high places that he had a sure-fire way that a school could tick all the boxes and so qualify for the programme.

He had found a place to set this up in Lucan, where he was minister. There was an old youth centre at the edge of town that was connected to his church, but to renovate it, and kit it out to a level that was needed, would cost a fortune. That's where Myles came in, not because he had a fortune (he most definitely didn't!) but because he had the visionary eyesight to think that it was more than just a hunch that God was behind this reconciliation process. Their next steps were logical, if you say them slowly!

Where would they get that kind of money? America. How would they convince some Americans to fund such an exotic project? You would have to go personally and ask them to invest. Who is free to go and do this? Myles and Phyllis – they had just finished a stint with Agapé in Germany. Who in America has that kind of disposable funds? Nobody knew, but Trevor had a few mates in the Presbyterian Church of the USA and some contacts in the American Ireland fund. By such inexorable logic Myles and Phyllis ended up based in Winter Park, Florida, for two years. By travelling to 22 states (and 'eating a lot of dinners') they unearthed Americans of goodwill (and they weren't all Irish-Americans) who were pleased to find a direct way to fund reconciliation during a time when others were still funding violence.

Once the Lucan side of the programme got going, you soon had school children from the North on carefully curated tours of the General Post Office in O'Connell Street – to tell the story of how the 1916 Rising began – and Kilmainham Jail, to tell how the Rising proceeded.

The tours included the obligatory stop at the river Boyne, leading one schoolboy from Ballymena, County Antrim, to exclaim, 'OK – I know that we won the Battle of the Boyne but how come they got to keep the river?'

Myles will tell you, to this day, that Florida was a long lesson in fund-raising. And the main thing he learned? – the donor has a greater need to give than the receiver has to receive. The money was found, the Lucan Centre got renovated and yes, kids from the North came to visit and were woven into the fabric of reconciliation. The Irish Department of Foreign Affairs awarded the Centre 'Project of the Year' in 1995 to commemorate the 50th anniversary of the United Nations. Meanwhile, in Myles's head, the seed of a wider, lifetime project was germinating. Of the three sibling couples, they would be the one that would do the hardest travel and attend the conferences in the scarcely-two-and-a-half-star hostels. The rest of the world had yet to feel the effect of Myles's missionary acumen.

CHAPTER 15

CRISS-CROSSING CULTURES

While Myles and Phyllis were doing their utmost to serve Ireland spiritually in the years of her 'Troubles', our European colleagues couldn't help but notice that Irish students and graduates were dispersing all over the globe in the cause of making Jesus famous for all the right reasons. So, they invited Pam and me to help to give this process a turbo-boost.

The idea was that since many young Irish people of our acquaintance had gone on short-term projects, we could coordinate their deployment, foster their welfare and upgrade their training. So far, they had gone to places like Zaire (as it was then called, now Congo), Bolivia, Algeria, and Poland. We could also provide the same service for other European graduates from the vantage point of a base in Germany.

We followed the logic and were happy with the idea of smoothing the way for our compatriots plus whoever else showed up. But first we would need to go through the exact same cross-cultural training as everybody else.

An eclectic group of veteran trainers had been assembled in the East End of London in the midst of the vast medley of cultures there. That's where the first four months of our new life would start.

In the meantime, I went down to ask the German Embassy in Booterstown in Dublin about a residence permit. I thought it was a simple transaction to say, 'We want to live in Germany,' but the consular official replied, 'That will be a temporary residence permit, then.' 'Oh, no,' I said, hoping he wasn't looking at us as a flighty case, 'We really want to live there.' But he knew how to sort the wheat from the chaff. 'Do you want to die in Germany?' 'Well, not really.' 'OK then, that will be a temporary residence.'

The day came. We packed up our stuff and, like so many before us, left Ireland. We didn't know for how long. It was February 1986. It could be for ever. You never know, do you? Before we made our way from Blackrock to the Dun Laoghaire-Holyhead ferry, our next-door neighbour did the kindest thing she could think of. She cooked us a full Irish breakfast to remember. It wasn't exactly the smoothest of crossings, so I had a few extra opportunities to savour that breakfast.

We ended up in Plaistow in the East End of London, bag and baggage, and were assigned to a flat conveniently located upstairs from the training room in the same building and in direct contact with local life. That building also backed on to a kebab shop which became a big part of our life because their back gate clanged loudly until late at night, reverberating through the house. In the morning we would find pickles strewn on the pavement because the kebab customers didn't seem to like the pickles that were included in their takeaway. Maybe they didn't have the heart to tell the proprietors face to face.

Language learning is a big deal when you're trying to identify with somebody's culture and it certainly was a big deal in our training. It's good manners and was exemplified by Christ himself. When he claimed to be the Son of God and foretold his arrest, death and resurrection he did so in a Galilean accent – and we know from the historical record that there was such an accent.

We were spoiled by having a phonetics expert on hand, Grace Liversage. Grace came from a background about as intercultural as you'd get. She was tutored in her childhood by Eric Liddell (the Olympic gold medallist whose life featured in the film *Chariots of Fire*) when they were both in a Japanese internment camp in China in the early 1940s.

I never grasped the significance of 'voiceless dental fricatives' like Grace would have wanted and thankfully the emphasis was on learning by *speaking*. The method is called LAMP (for 'Language Acquisition Made Practical'). Each of us trainees was assigned to a local person whose native language was not English. Pam got to spend time with a Gujarati lady who ran a corner shop – while she was running it. I was assigned to a Tamil guy called Chris. Somebody had failed to impress upon him that what I needed to do was learn to speak some Tamil. Instead, he thought it would be good for me to see Tamil script and revel in its wonder. He was right. It is beautiful indeed but the opportunity to *speak* Tamil passed me by.

While we busied ourselves with learning about cultures theoretically, we found that we were bumping into various cultures on a daily basis. One morning I opened the front door to find that a young, part-time homeless guy had ingeniously incorporated a hut made of pallet wood into our front entrance. As he saw our team clamber in and out of the building during the day, he knew that this wasn't an appropriate place to set up shop and moved his wood elsewhere – after telling us about his situation and how he got into it.

Language-learning wasn't the only training given. A good slice of time also went into maintaining your mental health. Here Dr June Morgan was drafted into service. She had served in Thailand and now, in retirement, was trying to help people who were going into the front end of the missionary process. I must say I baulked a bit when I saw on the schedule that she was going to give a 90-minute talk on depression. I even cheekily whispered to my classmates, 'Sounds depressing'. Even the global news was depressing. The nuclear reactor in Chernobyl in Ukraine had blown up on 26th April. Nine days later the city was evacuated, people in Britain were afraid of eating vegetables exposed to the radiation cloud and, for a few weeks nobody knew if anybody would be going anywhere, including aspiring missionaries.

The deadpan delivery of Dr June's talk was an inspiration. The first thing that struck me was her telling us that she did the *Times* crossword on the way out to us on the Underground. Apparently, she did the crossword every day, 'just to keep my mind straight'. She pulled no punches in explaining the danger zone we were sailing into by going into cross-cultural living. 'Everybody will experience some element of depression in their life,' she said, 'but missionaries are more susceptible.'

June illustrated this by recounting her distress in Thailand when she found her mother had died, long before the days of fast communication and travel. She turned herself in – to a psychiatrist based in the same hospital (who happened to be a Buddhist) who helped her, over time, to talk her way through it. Her message to us was as simple as it was brutal: (a) you will get depressed (b) watch out for signs (c) then go and see your doctor.

I went straight out to the local GP surgery after a quick bite of lunch. For weeks I had had some frustrating physical symptoms. There was a rash on my inner arm and what appeared to me to be a swelling in my groin. I had seen no medics, lived in denial and hoped it would all go away. The doctor on duty received me kindly, examined me and told me to come back in about a week. Next visit – same thing: examination, come back in another week.

On my third visit to the surgery they assigned me to yet another GP – this time an older gentleman. It was a cold day (the Spring of 1986 broke low temperature records) and I had my big coat on. I was still in the process of hanging it on a coat stand when he enquired, 'Have you by any chance, been subject to any kind of stress?' 'You haven't examined me yet; I'm just taking my coat off now'. He repeated his question, without a trace of irritation.

In my answer, I said two of the stupidest things I've ever said in my life; 'First, I'm a Christian, so I don't think stress is going to be an issue; and second, I'm just not that type of person,' He took some notes quietly, did a perfunctory inspection of my symptoms and gave me a prescription. 'Take one of these every day and we'll see how you do.'

I went back to the same doctor after only a few days to happily announce that the prescription had done the trick. All my symptoms, which had appeared unrelated, had gone, thanks to the little pill which had some kind of a jargon medical name when the pharmacist gave it to me. 'It's Valium,' said the doctor. 'Sometimes we use Valium diagnostically.' 'But how can that be?!' I persisted. 'How can a pill for my mind affect my body?' I'll never forget his parting words, 'You see, Mr Wilson, there is a strong connection between your body and your soul.' Dr Morgan had been right.

Of course, as you can guess, he also told me to 'take it easy'. Not as simple as it sounds. We were coming to the end of a strenuous three-month course, our sons were in a strange school, it was freezing cold, our previous landlady in Ireland had been writing to us arguing about our deposit and we were shortly going to move on to live somewhere (not sure where yet) in southern Germany.

But then I remembered something. There was a short-term solution waiting in the wings. The prescription at the pharmacy had not been totally used up! I went back and acquired the few remaining Valium, nipped out to a high-street travel agent and booked a very-last-minute cheap package holiday to the Adriatic coast of Italy for our whole family. Compared to the previous months I had a grand old time. Pam could see it – maybe even the boys. The seaside city of Rimini never looked so good.

Restored to better health, and with me hopefully gaining some humility, we graduated, shipped our things one more time, and took a flight to Basel on 30th June 1986. Now all we had to do was learn how to speak German.

Those thoughtful European colleagues had arranged a living situation for us which was as good as you'd get for language-learning, and that was now our daily focus. They found a Lutheran pastor, and his wife and family, who had a parish house (with an extension) big enough to accommodate all of us.

Having our whole family live inside their whole family was almost unheard of but it was a godsend for us. The couple, Traugott and Almut Fränkle, knew what we needed to do and went out of their way to help. They could both speak passable English, but they never did – just so we would be immersed in German. Now our language-learning had to be front and centre.

Our first task was for Pam and me to find a local person who would help us to say our introductory greetings. My helper taught me how to say a handful of short sentences which I then practised for a couple of hours before foisting myself on the general public around Betberg, our village. The LAMP method suggests you say your sentences to at least 30 individual people for two and a half hours every day. Since this would have been 20% of the population, I had to include an additional adjoining village.

The only person I could find there was a grave-digger working in the churchyard. You can imagine his thoughts when he looked up out of the grave only to see some fellow saying, 'Hello. My name is David. This is my third day here. I am learning German. Please correct me if I make a mistake.' And you can imagine my thoughts leaning down to speak to him.

But, as days turned into weeks and months, the eternally patient people of the Markgräflerland district taught us to speak as they did, including intricacies they don't tell you in books. Since German is one of those languages in which there are formal and informal ways of addressing people, I thought it would be simplest to learn the formal way first of all. Wrong.

I needed the informal to speak to the cat that wandered into the house. Similarly, you speak to your tummy with informal German (like when it rumbles and you say, 'You should take it easy there, tummy!'). Of course, neither the cat nor the tummy is worried about this, but your friends would find it highly entertaining to overhear you address your tummy formally, since there are two ways (formal and informal) of saying 'you'. German urban legend has it that chancellor Helmut Kohl told Ronald Reagan, 'You can say 'you' to me' (the legend is told with various potential characters in the roles). Legend it may be, but my heart went out to Kohl – or whoever it was.

Oddest of all, from my point of view, you addressed God only in the *informal*. That says something intimate about God's love for humankind. On the other hand, it was considered rude to address a migrant worker informally. I was significantly helped in all this by a weekend visitor to the parish house. He had a learning disability, spoke excellent German, and was Mr Sociable. I invited him to be my language-helper for the weekend, a task which he took on with great relish. My fledging attempts at speaking gave him a stream of entertainment and he gave me an education in pronunciation. Again and again was no problem.

That cross-cultural training we'd gone through in the East End was paying dividends, like 'Live with a family… Don't own a car…Don't introduce yourself with some high falutin' title…Always say "I am *learning* German" (or whatever language)…Meet your social needs in your new language.'

We were just getting into the swing of things when I had the sombre task of carefully constructing a new paragraph to say on the phone to Silvia, one of Pam's friends in our neighbourhood. I still have the little book in which I wrote it. In German, it says, 'Last week Pam's younger brother died suddenly. Unfortunately, he took his own life. So, Pam flew to California on Thursday for ten days. This Sunday she's coming back. When she comes it would be good for her to talk about it with friends. Do you think you could give her a call next week?'

Time stood still that week. Joel and Seán and I were stunned. Pam, who is unusually gifted in dealing with a crisis, served her family in California as only she could. Silvia *did* meet her after her return and did an exquisite job of comforting her with almost no words at all.

From our boys' perspective, two bad things had happened. Their uncle had died and their mother had gone away for a week and a half. On the Saturday night, the night before Pam's return, Joel said, 'Can you go to the supermarket and get some champagne?' It took me a while to work out what this was about – to say the least of it, we're not a big drinking family. He had worked out that since shops in rural Germany were not open on Sunday it would have to be Saturday. Then I asked him, 'Why champagne?' He had never tasted champagne – I don't know if he'd ever even seen it. His glorious, profound answer: 'Mum's coming home.'

CHAPTER 16

INTO THE TWO-THIRDS WORLD

The town of Müllheim, in the German state of Baden-Württemberg, was indeed fast becoming home for us. The building on the edge of the town, which was now to be our office, had been acquired from the SOS Kinderdorf organisation. They had previously established it as a home for war orphans after the Second World War. After Agapé eventually left, it was used to house 'Aussiedler' – ethnic Germans who were coming out from Russia as the Soviet Union's relationships with the West warmed up.

That cross-cultural training became a bigger part of our lives than we had expected – we were tasked with moving it from bustling London and hosting it in our modest, mono-cultural German town. That might feel 'cross-cultural' for some candidates, but we then needed to find ways that would beneficially challenge the German-speaking ones – because candidates came from all over.

The first group of candidates contained a surprise

package – my sister Ruth, her husband John McNeill and their one-year-old daughter Amy. Of course, we knew they were planning an overseas move but, as serendipity would have it, we all ended up in the same German town at the same time!

Most of those in the course were aiming to work in a stream of the movement that had two simple criteria: show a track record of making quality disciples and be good at a useful day job. John and Ruth fitted the criteria superbly. Behind them they had left a good track record of teaching in secondary schools in Northern Ireland – Ruth in Home Economics, John in Biology.

Not long after they arrived in Müllheim, John joined a group of friends who visited the nearby University of Basel (just over the Swiss border) and found a diverse range of students most of whom were ready to talk about Jesus. They looked for those who would like to meet again, to talk again – which is always the key to finding who is interested and who is faking it. The students came from Russia, India, Africa, North and South America, Iraq and Japan. One Chinese student surfaced who had heard of Coke, but hadn't heard of Jesus.

We had no Italians on the cross-cultural course in Müllheim. So, to get in some immersion language-learning practice, we moved the whole show to Florence for a week. We all jumped into that same process by which Pam and I had been learning German.

Another guest in our hotel in Florence, a businessman from Chicago, unwittingly encouraged us by an alarming remark he made about Italian people one day at breakfast, 'You'd think they would just make that little bit of effort and speak English.' I say he 'encouraged us' because, if any of us were wilting under the pressure of language learning, his comment made us steely determined that we were sure going to do better than that strange business guy!

The shock to the system delivered by learning a language appears in the duplicated letter which Ruth and John sent to their friends back in Ireland: 'On the first day we had a language helper teach us how to say, "This is my first day in Italy. I am learning to speak Italian. I have to say these phrases to 50 people. This is all I can say. Thank you for listening. Goodbye"…we were exhausted by the end of the week.'

John didn't regard himself as a 'natural fit' for language learning, but of course that was never a criterion. He dutifully learned his initial Italian phrases and set forth into an experience that was, for many of us, unnerving – but especially for John. By that evening he still hadn't clocked up his 50 contacts and went to bed discouraged. But such is the single-mindedness of the man that his resolve got the better of him, he got up again at 11:00 pm, dressed, and went round to the main Florence railway station which was nearby. There were enough passengers waiting for late-night trains to provide John with the last of his 50 chats. He slept much better that night.

That's one reason why, if you greet John in the Chichewa language today, he will answer you in a flash, because it was in the bush in Malawi that the McNeills' journey came to a stop. In that letter to their friends they had written, 'It feels odd that, as we are writing this, people in Africa are discussing our placement. We have no idea yet where we will be going.' Ruth and John were those dream-ticket candidates who had asked to be sent, 'wherever the need is greatest and we could fill that need'.

It wasn't lost on any of us that Bob Geldof, that great product of Dún Laoghaire, had already launched his work to wake the Western world to the plight of the 'Two-thirds World'. I had read his first autobiography *Is that it?* which would tug at anyone's heart-strings because he so despaired of meaning in his life. By the time of Live Aid in 1985, some meaning had returned, as he put the point so simply to the world-wide viewing audience, 'Give us the money!' But before long, Geldof realised that 'development', not just money, was needed. After another long while he felt compelled to add 'governance' too, since money and so-called development weren't going to work without ethics in governance – and in government too.

The McNeills' philosophy, and that of their Agapé co-workers, was disarmingly simple: 'There's a Saviour and it isn't me. And he isn't white either.'

John took on a teaching responsibility at Robert Blake Secondary School, located at Kongwe, in the middle of nowhere, set up by a South African philanthropist, Dion Retief. The then President of Malawi, Dr Hastings Banda, had designed a decentralisation system by which government departments and other functions would not congregate in the capital city of Lilongwe. In this, he was successful. A lot of things were in the middle of nowhere. At that stage health care was limited. There were seven dentists for a population of seven million people in a country with an area equal to the combined sizes of Scotland and Wales.

A couple of months ago I asked Ruth how our parents took it when they found out that she and John were going to Africa (and taking some of our parents' grandchildren with them). Her answer was quite illuminating:

'On the night that we told them – that was when they told us (and I don't know at what point they ever told you), "Well before David was born we prayed and said, Lord we would love to have children. If you give us children they're yours first and we have no particular ambition for their lives other than that they would know and follow you, but if you would call them into missionary service that would be our greatest delight."

'I'd never heard that before so that just blew us away. We were the culmination, you know – their boys had already gone. We were the last remaining.'

As they arrived in Malawi, Ruth (who had just given birth to their second baby daughter, Jem) was treated to a series of immunization shots – 11 of them in total! Their little family had just turned into a classical 'Irish missionary to Africa' family. They followed in a long and noble tradition. It felt all the more 'classical', but not at all comfortable, when they then headed into three consecutive months of stomach bugs, hepatitis, dysentery and malaria. The closest doctor was 35 miles away. Most of the language study went out the window.

John informed his Irish supporters that his biology room in the school 'has one gas tap but is well endowed with animal specimens – from elephant dung to a crocodile skull – and a bat which hangs above the blackboard'. Nor were animals confined to the biology class – Ruth met a scorpion in the bathroom. A more welcome visitor was a chameleon which had the capacity to 'eat 24 flies during one tea time'. There was even talk of mains electricity coming sometime soon.

By this time the McNeills already had 20 of the school students in Bible studies. By all accounts they were starting from a low base of Scripture knowledge, despite the fact that this area must be one of the most evangelised places in Africa. After all, the ground-breaking Scottish missionary, David Livingstone, came to Malawi in the 1860s. Seems like each generation needs to make its own decisions about following Jesus – or not.

I got to meet some of these students myself when I visited Ruth and John in December 1989. I had spoken at a conference in Swaziland and was determined that my route back to Germany would go through Kongwe, one of the most obscure districts in Malawi. It was obvious that the students held John in high regard. I sat at the back of his class one morning. First thing, one of the students had a question – more of a statement really. 'Sir, I wish to be called Christopher from now on, and not

'X Ray'. Apparently he had been born in a hospital with an X Ray department so the name 'X Ray' was quickly adopted by his mother for his 'English' name, to be used alongside his Chichewa name. John had to gently break it to him that he was so well known that there was little prospect of changing his name in his late teens. Now, decades later, there must be many an African teenage rapper who would be delighted to be called 'X Ray' – from birth!

I took the obligatory family photos, including my delightful nieces, who had known little more than local culture all their little lives, and headed back to another world in Europe. Later I learned that I had missed a lot of excitement. Not long afterwards, Malawi was rocked by two serious earthquakes in two days. John wrote, 'We were just settling back into bed after the second quake when there was a knock at the door. Some of the students had been injured…could we take them to hospital? We were concerned and then found out that their injuries were caused by jumping out of their hostel windows in the panic – without opening them first!'

Not long after the earthquakes, who should arrive in Kongwe but my parents, for a three-month visit. In talking to them afterwards, I got the impression that they settled into the new surroundings remarkably quickly, although I am certain that Ruth and John pulled out all the stops to ensure their comfort and protection (that year they had had five robberies in four months).

My father took to bush culture with alacrity for the

simple reason that he had white hair. At least, some of his hair was white – enough for him to be treated like royalty by the surrounding community. He went out for walks into the bush (the mind boggles at the implications) and was astounded at how everyone he met showed him such deference. Of course, he was a white man, and an old man, and a kind man, and Mrs McNeill's father – but he had never seen such deference in Strabane, nor in Newtownabbey, County Antrim where they now lived since he retired.

I was back in East Africa the next December, in Nairobi for a conference, and ran into Ruth in the oddest of circumstances. She was waiting at an open bus stop, with toddler Jem, being soaked to the skin by unseasonable, monsoon-type rain. I was speeding by in a car full of people. For a split second we recognized each other and thankfully she saw the funny side of the near-encounter as the car I was in continued at high speed, splashing her in the backwash. Thankfully, when we met at the conference she was still laughing.

Ruth, and many missionary women like her, never get properly recognized for their extraordinary accomplishments. Her 'home schooling' of Amy (then five years old), however warm and loving, was as formal as many a State school. That year she wrote to us, quite matter-of-factly, that Amy's curriculum now included such 'extras' as recorder, computer, French and letter-writing. All this was conducted while their two younger daughters, Jem and Lyn ,were running around the house.

'Lyn eats anything,' Ruth said, 'but has a preference for bugs – like cockroaches.'

The same year, Ruth reported that her handbag had been stolen from their car while she was momentarily distracted while she was packing their groceries on a visit to Lilongwe (the capital) – a visit then lengthened by a pointless afternoon sitting in a police station.

Later, in the same letter, 'the gardener killed two six-foot poisonous snakes in our garden, one of them hanging in the tree which gives shade to our girls' swings.'

That summer, which turned out to be the McNeills' last in Malawi, my parents visited again. It seemed like they couldn't get enough of Africa. When my father marched into the local clinic in Whiteabbey, County Antrim, to get his travel shots, the nursing staff were not best pleased because he had recently had a stroke. 'Are you sure, Mr Wilson? It's a long way away.' But nothing would put him off. 'What if something went wrong, Mr Wilson?' (which is the medical way of asking, 'What if you would die?'). My father assured them that 'they have great hospitals in Malawi.' They pursued with the unadorned question, 'What if you would die?' He knew the answer: 'They do great funerals.' 'Oh, Mr Wilson!!' they remonstrated. 'Don't worry,' said he, 'I'd have a great resurrection too.'

Neither hospital, funeral nor resurrection were necessary, although the senior Wilsons travelled some thousands of miles with John and Ruth which allowed them to be observers while John showed the *Jesus Film* to a thousand people in Livingstonia, in northern Malawi. On account of my mother's influence, they also got to drink a cup of tea in the café at the Victoria Falls Bridge.

John had got very busy in 1992, maybe realising that his time in Malawi was limited. He tried to get serious with some of the school students into whom he had poured his life as potential disciples. He wrote that his work was 'both exciting and depressing. My emotions can range from these two extremes in one day.' One key student had described himself as a 'processed Christian'. In John's view they were, 'boys who could win an Oscar' playing the part of "Christians". They had "Christian" parents, went to church and had been baptized as a baby…they saw baptism as a ticket to heaven.'

Again that summer John said he was 'sad and angry' because 120 people had been baptised in the local church. You might think that 120 was a good score but 'so many people were being confused and deceived into thinking unbiblical things' – like the 'ticket to heaven' idea. Life expectancy in Malawi being, at that time, in the low forties, you can understand their rush to get their ticket – and John's rush to make sure the ticket was paid for by Jesus, rather than a fake ticket manufactured out of religious mumbo-jumbo.

For his last big training session in rural Malawi, John secured the use of a tobacco-drying shed to accommodate the number of keen volunteer evangelists who planned to attend. It wasn't long before he realised that what these trainees were 'keen' on was mostly alcohol, since most of them turned up 'half-cut'. John switched to a very basic talk on how to get a complete life makeover from Jesus before you go out to try to persuade others to do likewise.

Back at Robert Blake School, he reckoned it was best to give his attention to the handful of boys who were determined followers of Jesus – and would one day become replacements for John. But there were also some irreplaceable people, in particular Benson the cook and Maria who worked in the house. Both of them had worked at Robert Blake for years and quickly transferred to John and Ruth when they arrived. For all four of them, it would be a funny old world without each other's company. Maria and Benson had become more like comrades in arms than just expats' employees.

Benson had become their key man in his village of Kadiwa where he took on the task of preparing a showing of the *Jesus Film* – a piece of adept organising that would always be beyond John's language capacity. After years of hearing the Christian gospel and a long time thinking about it, Maria trusted herself to Jesus one day after talking with Ruth in the house. During her time at Robert Blake, Maria had heard it all and seen it all. Ruth was so pleased that Maria would confide in her about this. By now she had become a close friend.

Maria had been estranged from her husband for four years because of his unfaithfulness and his taking a second wife. Her subsequent life had not been easy as she had to farm her own land, raise an eight-year old daughter, look after both her aging mother and grandmother. And, of course, hold down the valuable job of working for the McNeills.

Ruth wrote home, 'We want to help but do not know how to…and we don't know what to say. We can only love her and support her in this time of pregnancy and beyond. Last Christmas time her husband made an appearance for a few days. There was some sort of reconciliation between them. He left again, promising to be back soon. He died suddenly a few weeks later. Maria is now pregnant with his baby. This is difficult enough but is made more complicated by the fact that her husband probably had AIDS. He led a promiscuous life and in this part of the world this means that you are almost certain of being HIV positive.'

The news didn't get better soon. The next letter said, 'Maria may not be HIV positive' (not an encouraging way to say it). Then, 'the baby is overdue and has no weight gain'. You can understand everybody's elation when the following month, 'Maria's baby boy was born on 22nd November.' Maria named him '*Madalitso*' ('Blessings').

Now John's mind was on the McNeills' plan for a long visit to Belfast to report their work to those who had sponsored them. He felt like he had given Robert Blake all he could give and he told Ruth that he thought that some day God would want him to have a go at promoting the ultimate claims of Jesus at British universities. She laughed, 'No way am I leaving Malawi – or Africa!' It would be like moving from the bush to the jungle.

Back in Germany, after some 30 missionaries had

cycled through the course, Pam and I took a weekend break in the nearby Black Forest to pray and think about our own next options. It wasn't as if there was no more contribution to be made to the wide world – far from it. We just wanted to whittle down our choices to places where we could make a distinct difference. We narrowed it down to two – Hong Kong and Khartoum. We gently transported our two conclusions back to Müllheim to give them a strict mulling over. We had done less then a week of research when we were blind-sided by a new question put to us by the team leader of Agapé in the UK: 'What would you think of taking on my job? I'm tired.'

Had we listed all the conceivable countries to work in, this was one that would never have made the cut. But as we talked and prayed and thought about it, the idea became all the more striking – maybe because it seemed so bizarre. Hong Kong and Khartoum sank without a trace.

CHAPTER 17

LEAVING NO STONE UNTURNED

While the McNeill's gardener was busy killing dangling snakes in Kongwe, Pam and I, with our sons Joel and Seán, were gingerly getting used to a city that was new to us – Birmingham –blithely oblivious (pre-email) to any goings-on in Malawi.

We had previously regarded Birmingham as a place you see from the comfort of your own car on the occasions when you drive from the Stranraer ferry to London for some reason. You scarcely needed a reason to go to London, but Birmingham didn't present its most prepossessing side when you drove past it on the M6. That same M6 which ran so straight in beautiful Cumbria (courtesy of the Romans who originally built a straight road there) seemed to lurch to the left to avoid Birmingham, leaving you with only a view of what used to be its factories and obscuring the view of everything else.

But British Agapé was headquartered in Birmingham so we were going to live there. Of course, as soon as we arrived, the residents quickly brought us up to date: the city has 'more canals than Venice, more trees than anywhere else in Britain and more Pre-Raphaelite paintings than anywhere else at all'.

While we were still sorting out how best to approach Britain as a whole (if you can even do that) I decided that, on a personal level, I would give my attention to what I knew best. For me, that meant doing what I could to raise the profile of Christ in academia, particularly at Birmingham University. I met with the Christian staff group – both academics and admin people. My Agapé friend, Andy Moules, spent a lot of time with local students and I admired his spunky strategy. He attended a session of the university Jazz and Blues Society and chatted to the girl sitting beside him on the floor (apparently that's where you sat – on the floor leaning your back on the wall). He noticed that she was wearing a necklace with a little cross. 'I see you're wearing a little cross,' he remarked. 'Have you thought of maybe a little electric chair?'

'A what?!' the startled blues fan replied. 'Whatever for?' The redoubtable Andy explained that the cross was a particularly nasty method of Roman execution for insurrection – like, say, hanging or the electric chair or lethal injection in later times. Why, he wanted to know, had the culture gone mad about crosses when they represent such an ugly thing? What caused the big switch from 'execution symbol' to 'must-have logo'?

Andy knew, and the girl knew (and the dogs in the

street still know) that Jesus wasn't a militant dissident. There was a puzzle to solve. Andy left her with a broad hint that if millions of people, over so many years, hadn't been so utterly grateful to Jesus, maybe the cross would never have got as far as adorning her neck.

That puzzled girl's world-view wasn't unusual. The British culture needed help to blow away the dust and look into the raw material of basic information about the big questions in life. Too many students simply didn't know where to go to answer those questions. There was only one thing for it – invite help from Malawi. After only three months working in the UK I wrote to John and Ruth on 5th March 1992 :

'I have started and stopped and re-started this letter for a couple of months now. Let me explain. As soon as I got started here I thought to myself, "Boy, do I need help". Then the thought jumped into my mind, "Time for the McNeills"…

'As you know, we have often dreamed about the possibility of working together with you sometime in the future but now I am wondering how soon that sometime could be…

'I have turned over a lot of administration to somebody else. This has given me the sweet luxury of getting down to the real work I wanted to do, namely nose-to-nose evangelism with the 9742 students here – the jumper and jeans brigade – who are still asking daft questions and dying inside for the want of someone to lead them to Christ…

'Does Africa still badly need the gospel or can you help us here? Less than 10% of the population here goes to church. What's it like out there?'

Re-reading this correspondence in retrospect, it looks more than a little pushy. On 4th April I wrote to say, 'this strategy so excites me that I sometimes have difficulty going to sleep at night. I can see, as clear as daylight, the effect it would have upon our cultures. Sometimes I am a little impatient with those around me who do not necessarily see it so clearly. I tend to think they are asleep!' And on 17th November, 'Dear John and Ruth, We have your photograph sitting on the mantlepiece and we think about you and talk about you every day...'

I like to think that the McNeills were influenced by God's guidance, not just my pushiness. The upshot was that they wound up their operation in Malawi, said goodbye, for the time being, to Benson and Maria and transferred to the jungle of UK academia. John arrived in Birmingham in the aftermath of a 'Christian Week' which had just been conducted at the university.

Departments and student societies had been invited to mark the week with topics in the context of the normal curriculum, along with events hosted by the societies. Ten visiting lecturers from other UK universities addressed over 600 students about Christian implications in a wide range of university disciplines. The Debating Society sponsored a debate on 'This house believes that God has the Answer'. Gordon Wilson (no relation) accepted an invitation to come from Enniskillen, County Fermanagh, at his own expense, and tell an enthralled audience about his peace campaign.

Gordon's daughter Marie had been killed in the 1987 Enniskillen bombing. He made no secret of the fact that it was his faith in Christ which allowed him to pursue a path of forgiveness for the perpetrators. Three months after his Birmingham visit he accepted an appointment to the Irish Senate to promote his message to an even wider arena.

A 'National Student Belief Survey' was launched, starting in Birmingham, so I volunteered to be an interviewer. One of the first people I met in the process was a student from Brighton. I had been visiting the university's Barber Institute of Fine Arts – a favourite getaway spot with important Pre-Raphaelite paintings. We fell into conversation and she kindly answered the survey questions. When I asked the last question, 'If you could know God personally would you be interested?' her answer was, 'I just quit the church.' 'Really?' 'Yes, I disagreed with some of their policies.'

This was the first time there had been any talk of church (which formed no part of the survey). I pointed out that just as there are physical laws (like gravity) that govern the physical universe so there are spiritual principles which can guide our relationship with God. 'Exactly!' she burst out, 'That's what I want to do! I want to find those spiritual principles of the universe!' She said her first step would be to investigate what each of the world's great spiritual leaders had said. I told her that this was always a useful idea and recommended that she take particular notice of any leader who rose from the dead – like in the Bible.

CHAPTER 18

MAKING A MARK

John McNeill is a fast learner and gave his undivided attention to listening to students. Early on he met a student who, with a single comment, established a lodestar for John's time in Birmingham. John and Martyn had met over a Mexican meal in the Guild of Students (Students' Union) and when John asked him what he wanted to do with his life he simply said, 'To make a mark'. That became John's rallying cry and in the process he advised Martyn that he could do no better than follow Jesus who always leaves a mark. This Martyn proceeded to do. Soon he was helping to organise John's projects – like taking a group of his new UK friends back to Malawi for a month in the summer of 1995.

John was delighted to bring them to the university of Malawi in the city of Zomba where they enjoyed talking with a couple of hundred students. Alerted by John's previous experience they avoided religious talk like the plague and stuck with wide-ranging discussions about the historical person of Jesus of Nazareth.

But this Malawi visit had a bittersweet side to it. John

fitted in a visit to Robert Blake and the old friends there. But two were missing – Maria and Benson. They had simply been claimed by the low life expectancy. John was gutted. Ruth later told me that when she heard Maria was gone she vowed never to go back to Malawi – it was just too painful.

John's feelings were all the more conflicted when, in the midst of this time in Malawi, my father (his father-in-law) was moved from a nursing home in Glengormley to a local hospital where he died very soon afterwards. John (and Ruth) wanted to be in two places at once. It was not to be.

The McNeills' Birmingham life was fractured by such life-crises. The next year they felt the pull of Africa again and went into preparation mode to be missionaries in Eritrea, somewhere they had, for a long time, dreamed of working. John reversed out of various accumulated responsibilities in the UK and began to plan meticulously for Eritrea.

But, while they were still in Birmingham, the wheels came off. He lost over three kilos in weight in short order. Ruth noticed. Then one day I got a phone call to say that John was experiencing serious psychological burnout and had to take time off, with immediate effect and for an indeterminate length of time. It was months before we heard from John again – this time in a letter to his friends:

'At last I am able and want to write this letter. These last months have not been easy. In fact they have been both painful and humbling; not the sort of thing one chooses to go through…What I have gone through is best described as "burnout", the symptoms of which, for me, were high levels of stress, manifesting itself in irregular sleep patterns, loss of appetite and feelings of heaviness and sadness. I'm told these are also signs of reactive depression.

'I had never thought this could happen to me – how wrong I was! …I needed to "down tools" and walk away from everything and everybody – otherwise the damage could be long-term and a lot worse.

'During this time of retreating it was just Ruth and I with the Lord; few others got a look-in…I know that many things helped to cause my burnout but I feel that the main factor was that I let my heart shrivel up.'

My own thoughts raced back to the training that I had gone through with Dr June Morgan those years before, 'Missionaries are more susceptible to depression. They put themselves in harm's way.' Should I have noticed John's difficulties earlier? Should I have intervened? He was my brother-in-law after all.

While John recovered, his circumstances did not. His mother was diagnosed with liver cancer and given a few weeks to live. They asked me to speak at her graveside. I said that if Jesus cried when his friend Lazarus died it's OK for us to do the same. Then the Eritrea plan collapsed. Remarkably, John and Ruth took all this in their stride. To everyone's amazement (not least mine) they communicated with their African friends and found a very different place to serve – recruiting a new generation of university students to be enthusiasts for Jesus in the almost new country of Namibia ('four times the size of the UK with a population the same as Northern Ireland').

A lot of people were thinking what I was thinking – 'How come John had a "burnout" followed by a string of crises and now thinks he'll be OK in Africa again?' John was ready for us. In his next letter to close friends he wrote, 'Since my burnout two Easters ago I have learnt much about myself, life and how my job affects my health. God is still in the business of recycling people and events. I am testimony to this.' This version of John was a lot wiser than the previous one.

You could see it in their way of life. As soon as they were established in Namibia they didn't take 'work calls' on the weekend. Maybe because of his more balanced life, John was called upon by various third-level institutions to give orientation talks to students about subjects like 'spiritual wellness'. From early on, he decided that it was better for him to wait for committed students to arise and take on the mantle of leadership, than for John to do it all himself. They spent twice as long in Namibia as they did in Malawi. Maybe that speaks for itself.

Family became a bigger thing than it ever was. They reported, 'It's good for students to see how a Christian family operates (albeit an Irish one). A lot of them come from broken, dysfunctional, sometimes polygamist families, so they don't have a clear idea of what a

Christian family can look like. They saw us – warts and all.' They took time off. My mother went to see them and they took her (again!) to see the Victoria Falls. Ruth says, 'When I see a bridge like the Victoria Falls Bridge on the border between Zambia and Zimbabwe I think, "This will help relations between the two countries." John thinks, "Bungee-jumping!" ' And bungee-jump he did – all 111 metres of it!

Ruth and John kindly let me read their correspondence that covers these years. By the time they finished in Namibia they had moved to digital communications and copies were no longer kept. So I find it poignant that John's last hard-copy letter says, 'Ruth was woken at 4 a.m. with a thief at the foot of our bed. He stole my laptop.'

CHAPTER 19

UNLIKELY BIBLE HEROES

After John's 'burnout' time, he and Ruth had been uniquely able to add value to that cross-cultural training because we had now moved it to Birmingham and they had fresh experience to share. Some good friends I had first met in Swaziland, Larry and Eea Platner, came to run it – except now the clientele was different. This time our context was the Sparkhill district, a true amalgam of cultures and an ethnic centre of gravity for Pathans – the very people we never got to live with in Pakistan. Soon we had a keen Malawian on the training course, Haswell Beni, an earlier graduate of Robert Blake school (of all places!). He was limbering up to become a missionary to Italy.

Being your typical individualistic Westerner, I was interested to find out what age Haswell was as we got to know each other. He didn't know. He wasn't particularly bothered either – until he and his wife Maria went to the bank to apply for a mortgage. The bank was very interested. So Haswell called his father who did a concentrated mental work-out to think through which year Haswell was born – was it the year before or after the bad harvest? Thus equipped with a rough idea of the year Haswell cheerfully decided his own date of birth – and he still has it to this day!

Even the communication between Haswell and his father amazed me. He later told me that as soon as mobile phones became common Haswell made sure his father had one. When Haswell would call from Europe, his Dad would hang the phone on a tree in his village in Malawi, with the speakerphone switched on, and the extended family and friends would sit under the tree to listen. I wish I could do that with my family and my phone!

Haswell was one of a growing number of people who must live in two cultures at once. When he went back for a visit to his family in Malawi he took the opportunity to seek out his old friends from Robert Blake School to see where they had ended up in life. Upon his return to the UK he told me, rather soberly, that many of the friends were in high-level government jobs. I wondered what was so sober about that? Then he told me, 'These guys had the one qualification the government was looking for.' 'What was that?' I enquired. 'They were alive,' he said. 'All the guys from school who had messed around sexually were dead because of AIDS.' Now, *I* was the one that felt sober.

Little did we realise it, but yet another course in culture awaited us, hidden in plain sight. I received a letter one day from an old friend whom I only vaguely knew in Germany. He had spent years befriending asylum applicants in Germany, especially Iranians, and he told me there was, right there in the Birmingham area, a keen believer who had had to escape from Iran because of his unbending loyalty to Jesus in the face of government disapproval. Apparently he was now working incognito in a pizza place.

I asked Larry to check out this somewhat way-out story. Larry found the pizza shop, and also found the Iranian who was understandably suspicious of an inquisitive stranger showing up out of nowhere. Larry worked hard to find common ground. He suggested some names in Christian leadership that he and the pizza man might mutually know – but these names drew a blank. No progress was made until he mentioned international-level leaders in the Christian faith that he happened to know. Bingo! – Mr Pizza knew them too. Now he (let's call him 'Javad') was more excited than Larry.

Javad's excitement was expressed in the only language he had – Farsi. Over the months that followed he explained to Larry, in still halting English, how he and his wife ('Sahar') had got to where they were. Christian leaders in Iran had felt under pressure, such that Javad feared for his life. So, he took an unusual step to deal with that – he disappeared. Into thin air. One day he was there, the next he was gone – gone into an underground network of travel that would take him through much of the Middle East and a lot of Western Europe. Back in Teheran, Sahar worked out what to do. She shut up shop completely and took their children with her to the UK where she had sufficient family connections to allow her to travel there. True to her calculations, Javad turned up.

That sounded like an exotic and dangerous journey, but more was to come, because they now wanted to talk about their future. Javad had a list and it sounded like the most outlandish of shopping lists. In order, he wanted to: learn English, find enough sponsors who would understand his plan (which he regarded as a God-given plan), then leave the pizza business (his only source of income) and then launch full-time into an operation of holding out a hand of friendship, as a devout follower of Jesus, to Muslims in Britain. He had a special sympathy for Iranians who were arriving for all sorts of motivations – all of them desperate enough to undertake the most perilous of voyages.

They put this plan to me and I took a deep breath. But I reckoned they deserved the same dignity as anyone else who felt he heard God's call, so an interview was set up to help Javad and Sahar decide if this was truly God's idea – and to help us, their new friends, decide if we should play a part in helping them. Even the circumstances of the interview were incongruous. For starters, where would we find a Farsi translator? Amazingly, we found the right woman in Frances who appeared out of the Sparkhill woodwork. She had been helping in the cross-cultural training and was bi-lingual in English and Dari, which is an Afghan dialect of the Farsi language. Odd, too, was the setting for the interview – a meeting room in an industrial estate in Tysley in Birmingham where, once upon a time, they made brake linings for virtually every British car in production.

Although Frances's help in the communication process was obviously vital, we could already sense that this Iranian couple had the bit between their teeth, and in the nicest way. There was nothing arrogant about them, but they had that quality that told us they'd seen everything and now they wanted to make their lives count in a big way. So we said (still all through translation), 'Let's do this!'

It didn't all come true overnight. But, one by one, Javad's shopping list was fulfilled. The last was the money. Just as he was finding sponsors, their family had another unanticipated crisis. The landlord of their house decided to sell it, which would leave the family back near square one. Javad decided that to continue his new work he needed to buy the house himself even though he didn't have anything near a deposit. He told the rest of the family to pray.

As the sale deadline approached, he got up one morning and found an envelope that had been pushed through the letterbox. On it was written, 'From God for the house'. He brought it into the kitchen where they were having breakfast so they could open it together. They spread out its contents on the kitchen table – £5,000 in notes, just what they needed to nail the deal. They cried. We lived quite nearby. They told us about it. We cried too. If that bizarre interview had needed one more twist to confirm our plans, that was it.

Today you will meet men and women in many a British city for whom that 'hand of friendship' has been a life-saver. Javad is known throughout Muslim and Christian circles as a man whose belief in God is deceptively simple and amazingly influential.

Javad's most ardent champion was another co-worker in the Birmingham area, John Arkell, who had long been poring over the issue of countering the national information deficit about Jesus.

Javad wasn't John's only enthusiasm. He couldn't get out of his head the idea of an information video that could be nationally distributed. That kernel of thought that he had carefully nursed began to germinate as the 1990s went on, for the simple reason that the 1990s were, unavoidably, going somewhere. And that 'somewhere' was the year 2000, which would be, in our lifetime, the ultimate public birthday of Jesus.

While the rest of the world was worrying about whether programmers could get their computers to recognise a new century (computers had never met a new century before), John was quietly recruiting a band of half-a-dozen or so experts – some in publishing, some in logistics, some in writing, some in PR. They wanted to see if the *Jesus Film* could be committed to video and supplied, at a ridiculously low price, to enough volunteers to cover every district in the country in the year that enveloped the turn of the century.

John's team had crunched the numbers and knew

how many British homes had a video-player (24 million) and had even tested the percentage of homes on the average street that would take a video. By October 1999 they had distributed 150,000 videos and they knew they needed to order hundreds of thousands more. Graham, their logistics man, got the job of negotiating with the Kodak company to get high-quality copies at the best price.

Initially Kodak wouldn't budge, and it turned out that they also had contracts to copy the *Jesus Film* for other countries. So Graham proposed a new contract – that Kodak provide all the millions of Jesus videos needed to supply the whole world. Needless to say, the price dropped. I think that the Kodak guys were still shaking their heads in bewilderment after signing. They later went out of business – but I don't think we were the reason!

Church members of every conceivable flavour and colour, 12,000 of them, collaborated at a local level. There was a certain communal satisfaction that at last they had found something they could totally agree on – showing the public their ultimate hero. And it wasn't that simple – it wasn't like delivering pizzas. Each household, door to door, was offered the video for free with the deal that they would give their opinion of it when the distributors called back a week later. And they visited 1,800,000 homes.

By the end of the year 2000 the number of households with the Jesus video had risen to 400,000 and a further

100,000 more were added during the next six months. John's Millennium team eventually reckoned that the number of homes offered a video was the equivalent of all of Scotland! Of course, not all the households visited were in Scotland, but it correctly gave us the impression that the number was simply *big*.

Included in that enormous number of viewings there were myriad personal stories. Thirty students living at the Indian YMCA, round the corner from our flat, ordered videos for themselves. One of the distributor groups wrote our team a note to say, 'A Muslim hairdresser cries every time she watches the Jesus video and insists that her clients watch it while she does their hair!'

These heroes of distribution were far from the first British people to be so minded. Indeed, our time in England served as a crash-course in the story of Bible pioneers. The first we noticed was the case of William Tyndale. Near where we lived, the British Library was running an exhibition to mark Tyndale's 500th anniversary, by giving access to see the work for which he lost his life – translating the Bible from the Greek and Hebrew in which they were written into the language of everyman. This activity was regarded as suspicious by the great and powerful who seemed to think that if the average citizen got their hands on a readable Bible goodness knows what would happen next.

To begin with, I was delighted that the library could produce three copies of Tyndale's New Testament still extant. I was further amazed about the size of the thing –

it measured three by ten by fifteen centimetres. It could have easily fitted into my jacket pocket. Apparently this was deliberate. They were all that size because they were dangerous contraband that had to be smuggled into England from the Low Countries, hidden in bales of hay. Another surprise was that the library had a copy belonging to Anne Boleyn, the second of Henry VIII's six wives, and she had made some tiny notes in the margins. Anne didn't last too long thereafter, having failed to produce a male heir.

As for Tyndale, let's just say that he was not one of Henry's favourite writers. Sir Thomas More, Henry's chancellor, described him as 'a hell-hound in the kennel of the devil'. In an early book-burning frenzy Tyndale Bibles were thrown into a bonfire in central London. He himself had had to do his work at a distance, in Germany. Once his translation was finished, a printer in Cologne started the presses rumbling but vandals broke in and stopped them before the first Gospel, St Matthew, was finished.

Not a man to be daunted, Tyndale moved his whole operation again and his completed books eventually came off the press in the German city of Worms – for secret shipping up the Rhine. But it cost him his life. He was tracked down near Brussels, betrayed by a compatriot and burned at the stake on 6th October 1536. By that time, he had generated 83% of the words that went on to be the 'King James Bible' seventy years later, including many expressions that have ended up in modern English, like 'the powers that be' and the 'signs of the times'.

No decent exhibition is complete without a gift-shop and, as we hastened through it, one book called out, 'Buy me, buy me!' It was none other than a Tyndale New Testament, the first complete reprint since 1526, same 'spellyng', same small size. That's how I know it fits in a jacket pocket!

Then I found the case of an even earlier Bible hero in Leicestershire. We were attending a conference in Lutterworth when somebody said this was where John Wycliffe was from. Wycliffe had organised a translation of the Bible from a Latin version into (then) contemporary English. The same problem arose with which Tyndale later had to contend. The 'powers that be' didn't like it, nor did they much like Wycliffe. What is it with totalitarian regimes that the Bible annoys them so much? Maybe, at the heart of it, it's simply the indignity of finding out that you're not top dog in the universe. Certainly Wycliffe was keeping up the pressure about the Bible being the ultimate authority.

He died of a plain ordinary stroke in 1384. No burning at the stake for him. However, after his death, such was the vitriol against him that officialdom decided he was a heretic and decreed that he be exhumed, his body burned, the bones ground to dust and thrown into the river, so nobody would ever hear of him, or indeed think of him, again. So, in 1428 (forty-four years later!) the dust was thrown into the river Swift.

That river was no more than a couple of miles from our conference centre so in May 2003 (another 575 years later) I went down there, to the area where the dust-throwing took place and took a photograph, just for 'divilment'. I showed it to the conference and John Wycliffe *was* thought of again.

Yet another spot in the English Midlands introduced us to the work of another heroic Bible person, none other than William Wilberforce, who is best known today as the man who worked for the abolition of slavery. Pam and I were driving down the M6 and noticed the sign for 'The Potteries'. We thought it would be rude to pass by this opportunity to see the exhibition of beautiful Wedgwood pieces. Everything in that show is beautiful, except one piece. That is a pottery cameo, designed by Josiah Wedgwood himself, depicting the plight of an African slave in chains. It was commissioned by Wilberforce and his political friends as a keepsake to be circulated to those who could vote against slavery.

An inscription on the cameo says, 'Am I not a friend and a brother?', based on the teaching of the Bible, in the book of Acts, in which the apostle Paul told the Greek philosophers in Athens that 'all nations of men' had one origin. The cameo became a runaway hit, the inscription became the campaign slogan, and it was reproduced by the thousand. Benjamin Franklin ordered a consignment for Philadelphia, and soon they were the symbol for American abolitionists too. They became a fashion statement, even worn as bracelets and as hair ornaments.

There was never any doubt about Wilberforce's driving motivation. When he had decided to make the following of Christ his guiding North-star he even wondered about staying in politics. A chat with John Newton, author of *Amazing Grace* and a former slave-ship captain, convinced him to stick with it. Wilberforce's devotion to Christ was obvious, in private and in public, throughout the weary, forty-year long parliamentary march to abolition.

One is forced to wonder if he ever got any spare time. If he did, he didn't waste it. Among his many humanitarian interests he was also a founder of the Bible Society in 1804. Originally, it was brought to his attention that it was hard to find an affordable Bible in Wales. Wilberforce thought, 'We can't have that!' and, once that issue was addressed, he thought, 'Why not the rest of the country? And why not the rest of the world?' The Bible Society is now represented in 200 countries, distributing millions of Bibles every year in over 100 languages.

That visit to Wedgwood wasn't my last brush with Wilberforce. A few years ago I was asked to organise a tour of London for an international conference that was meeting there. The cheapest and most efficient way to transport a conference roomful of delegates was to hire a big red London bus. Our tour was to include Wilberforce's home area of Clapham Common. He, and a posse of campaigning Christian friends, organised to live in houses around the Common so they could support each other in their various public-spirited causes, often chewing the fat, praying, and studying the Bible late into the night.

That green space is just as pleasant today and Holy Trinity church, which Wilberforce and company attended, is still there, to the north end of the Common. I had asked if we could meet the present minister, David Isherwood, who kindly turned up and opened the building. Some of our delegates just wanted to sit in a seat, any seat, that Wilberforce may have sat in.

Meanwhile, I was wandering around the outside of the church with the minister. We were soon talking about modern slavery and whether it is worse now than in the 18th century. 'The key question is,' he said, 'who made the shirt on our back?' What a good question. Wilberforce would have liked that question. When I went home, I took off my shirt and checked the label. The answer was not good.

Those 18th century men and women were made of sterner stuff. Sterner than me anyway. And none sterner than William Carey, another Bible man whose place I stumbled on during yet another conference in the Midlands. I was vaguely aware that this intellectual giant of Indian fame came from the Northampton area. I say 'Indian fame', for it was in India that he spent 40 massively productive years during which he oversaw the translation of the Bible into over thirty languages. Before he left England Carey had reckoned that when Christ said, 'Go into all the world and preach the gospel,' he wasn't joking. So, he totted up the available estimates to enable him to count all the people on earth and he published the results as a stimulus to others to spread the gospel more evenly.

When I got to that part of Northampton, I asked around and found Carey's cottage in the village of Moulton, still standing, beside the 'Telegraph' pub in West Street. It is still hard to imagine that this was the source of such erudition, zeal and passion – all expressed by a man who was a cobbler by trade and also tried his hand at some school-teaching. Immediately round the corner there was also the Baptist church in which he preached.

The church was still operating, and they had someone, Margaret Williams, specially designated to show visitors around, which she did with understandable pride. One wall had a mural depicting the many aspects of Carey's life. No wall could truly do it justice. I gazed at it all, took in what I could and signed the visitors' book. That's when I noticed that the person immediately before me had come from Bengal to see this little building.

It needs to be said that Carey was not exactly a tool of British imperialism. He was, in fact, a thorn in the side of the East India Company. His very presence made them queasy because they were morally offended at his Bible emphasis since it had implications about how they went about their (questionable) business. And they didn't like the close contact he had with Indians (it was closer than theirs) because they thought that it would lead to unrest.

They, too, had realised that reading the Bible might give a person the impression that all men were equal. Their simple solution – throw Carey out of British-Indian territory, which explains why he actually operated near Calcutta (Kolkata) and maybe explains too why he never returned to English soil. Carey paid dearly for living such a pioneering life. His first wife, Dorothy, suffered from poor health and died there. He also buried his second wife, Charlotte. His third wife, Grace, was the one who ended up looking after him in his declining years.

Carey was the person who brought the first printing-press to India. He published the first newspaper. He learned and translated scriptures into Bengali, Oriya, Marathi, Hindi, Assamese and Sanskrit. No surprise then that Carey's expertise in languages resulted in his being appointed a professor at the university. He also had an intense interest in botany and eventually earned wide respect as probably India's greatest botanist, resulting in another university appointment.

Note that Sanskrit is also the language of the Hindu scriptures. Carey knew how to spend time humbly at the feet of the pundits in order to learn Sanskrit and then return the favour by giving them, through Sanskrit, the good news about Jesus Christ. Even signing that visitors' book gave me a tiny vicarious feeling of identification with this giant influencer and put a spring in my step.

CHAPTER 20

'YOU OWE ME FIVE DOLLARS'

We had long since learned that our British co-workers needed no lectures from me about the spiritual obligation to be net contributors to the world, like these heroes of earlier times. Pam and I weren't the only ones to have caught the international bug. Some of them (including Ruth and John) had caught a serious dose. For solidarity's sake we had decided that all of our UK leadership team would go together to see what we could make of that global siren song.

The eight of us in the motley crew that comprised that 'leadership team' were united in one thing. We wanted to do what we could to connect with a group of people who had very limited opportunity to access Bible information. So, we were aiming for an 'unreached people group'. We had a hunch we'd find them in Kalmykia, the only republic in Europe with a majority Tibetan Buddhist population. In fact, we had a number of hunches, but that was the first. This was to be a reconnaissance visit – to find the best place for a long-term team. Along with

Pam and me were Phil (musician – the photographs show him wearing a tie), Rod (bit of a mystic), Dave (computer man), Chip (manager), Diane (counsellor) and Ed (bad golfer). Like I said, we were a motley crew. First stop was to be Rostov-on-Don.

Although we did a fair bit of flying on that day in April 1993 we felt like we spent a good part of it in minibuses, first of all between two Moscow airports – Sheremetyevo and Vnukovo, and then from Rostov-on-Don airport to the imaginatively named 'Hotel Tourist'. On this latter journey we were accompanied by an attentive translator, who had met us at the airport. Halfway there we were stopped by a police car because they thought our driver had cut in too smartly in front of them (never a clever driving manoeuvre with police anywhere). My diary says that they had an exchange of 'intemperate words on both sides'. After a pause, the translator delivered the meaning of this long and sometimes vitriolic tirade by saying two words: 'An argument'.

Rostov-on-Don was meant to be a staging post for visiting Kalmykia. Dave got busy working on the necessary bureaucracy and the rest of us had a good look at Rostov. Not only was everything new to us but we, as Westerners, were new to them. Through our translators' contacts we were whisked away to visit a children's hospital. We marvelled at the kindness they showed both to the children and to us. On leaving they showered us with a bewildering assortment of gifts – hand lotion, packs of postcards, an Easter cake, some boiled eggs and a vinyl record of six Bach violin concertos.

The head of the school of journalism had organised our next visit (apparently intended to increase our knowledge of Rostov). She wanted us to address her students. Although they were entering into a 'new Russia' she said, 'The country's social and political systems are bankrupt.' A journalist from the daily Rostov newspaper seemed to confirm her analysis. When we got a chance to chat, he told me, 'I desperately want to follow the Lord but I am pressurized to print things that I doubt are true, about economics – and that's my speciality.'

Eventually Dave, who was doing the hard yards with bureaucracy, came back and reported, 'It's not going to work for us to travel to Kalmykia, so we are going to the city of Ufa. That is our next option. It's another two time zones away.' In a nine-hour grind of office work somewhere, Dave surrounded himself with a confetti of paperwork, re-routed our Aeroflot tickets through Ufa, arranged our visas for Ufa and retrospectively registered us with the Rostov city authorities for permission to stay in the hotel we were now leaving after three days.

About the only thing we knew about Ufa was that the ballet dancer Rudolf Nureyev began his dancing career there – not much to go on. So, back to the airport and off we flew to Ufa (that wonderful city even *sounds* somehow ethereal).

These were the days which seasoned travellers refer to as the 'old Aeroflot'. We were being hosted by the 'Intourist' travel agency. This sounded fine until the plane landed and everybody stood up to reach for their bags. But then the cabin crew said, 'All Russians sit down again!' Apparently that was how they sorted out the international tourists from the locals. Our team, at this point, sticking out like a sore thumb, then realised that the best way we could help the now-sitting, glowering Russians, was to get off the plane as swiftly as possible so they could be released.

We were clearly directed to go and enjoy the Intourist lounge while our paperwork was being processed. The airport even provided a neatly uniformed staff member to greet us at the said lounge. Her greeting lives on in the memory to this day because she opened lips adorned with the reddest lipstick roubles could buy and said, 'You owe me five dollars.' It appeared that each of us owed her five dollars.

Before long, Diane twigged what the problem was and spent the next twenty minutes or so gently teaching the greeter the subtle difference between saying, 'You owe me five dollars,' and 'Good afternoon – there is a five-dollar charge for the use of the lounge.' The airport HR department had been a bit stingy on supplying language training for their staff. According to the visitors' book an American political personage had gone before us and he was less than complimentary about Miss Redlips and her greeting.

Dave and I were then directed to the man who would process that paperwork, which sounded like a routine task. However, the man into whose office we were ushered was the Aeroflot manager whose job it was to represent the FSB (in former times known as the KGB). 'This is not a visa,' he started. 'Your piece of paper is simply a written statement by some businessman in Rostov saying that he thought it would be a good idea for you to visit Ufa. What we need from you is a piece of paper from some notable person in Ufa who is inviting you to visit them.' Now that I think of it, he was very gracious, speaking to us clearly, with no malice.

After meditating on the blankness on our faces for a while he said, 'You can stay, but bring me the right paper. Tomorrow.' Then he stamped our papers, and went off to interrogate somebody more interesting. (In the end it took us a full three days to procure the 'right paper' from a suitably notable person and we went out to the airport, a little nervously, to present it to the manager. We left it at his office – he wasn't even there – and we never heard another word about it.)

Later in the day, Rod's friend Vova arrived from St Petersburg and joined us in our downtown hotel, yet another 'Hotel Tourist'. Vova's job was to prevent us from making really silly mistakes and to use his Russian charm to help us get more done than normal people would do in the time available.

We were feeling buzzed, having 'escaped' the FSB and wanted to see what this town was all about. Eagle-eyed Rod spotted a bus at the terminus opposite our hotel and got Vova to ask the driver, 'Are you finished for today?' Vova mentioned that when he was finished we would be glad to pay him a good number of roubles to show us the city's landmarks. The rouble had recently suffered its most serious collapse which meant that we could probably have afforded to pay his month's wages.

Suddenly the driver remembered that he was finished, and Rod called out to us, 'Everybody get on board!' Thus we got a late afternoon guided tour of Ufa taking in the Bashkortostan parliament building, the TV station and Pushkin Street where the Institute of the Arts was headquartered.

Then we were treated to the driver's favourite – an enormous cast iron statue of a famous Bashkir war hero, Salawat, on his prancing horse, holding a whip in his hand. Salawat had fought against Catherine the Great in 1774 and came to represent Bashkir exceptionalism as they were later to become the first republic to gain autonomy in the Soviet Union (in 1919).

Just as we arrived, a high-level four-man delegation from Kazakhstan turned up comprising one Kazakh, one Russian, one German and one in-charge Bashkir. We got the impression that the Kazakh was being respectfully dragged around a well-worn tourist trail.

It wasn't hard to wake up in the morning with such a tantalising feast of lessons to learn about Bashkir life and culture. We decided to put a bit of shape on our reconnaissance of Ufa, so after breakfast we read together the story of the first ever missionary journey (which was to Cyprus). The journey is recorded in the *Acts of the Apostles* in which the missionaries, Paul and Barnabas, ended up talking to the governor, Sergius Paulus. The text points out that Sergius was 'an intelligent man' and he soon became a believer in Jesus.

Thus fortified, and also sure that Ufa had many intelligent leaders, we divided the various national institutions between us. I went to call on the Minister of Education only to be told by his secretary that it was impossible to see him. I thought, 'Oops, it looks like I'd need an introduction and there's a three-month waiting list.' But the Minister's inaccessibility had a simpler explanation. He was just having his lunch.

Dave and I went to see Mr Mansurov, the technical director of the national television station – no need for an appointment there either. Ed and Phil called on the vice-principal of the university.

Rod and I went to visit 'School 35' on Gafuri Street – a school for the children of elites which taught through the medium of English, making it almost a national institution all on its own. The school was quite appropriately round the corner from the giant Salawat statue. The director, Grigori Simeonovich, a veteran of the 'Great Patriotic War', had built up the school from scratch, 40 years before.

He received us cordially and showed us the wonders of '35', bursting with understandable pride. 'We even have a clinic downstairs to deal with all kinds of common diseases. We can even perform simple operations.' Somehow he noticed that I had a little mole on my eyelid and nothing would please him more than for me to go downstairs to the clinic to have it removed. I found the politest way I could to show how keen I was to stay upstairs.

Undaunted, the director then invited us to an early lunch, which we accepted. We were assured we would have the same menu as the rest of the school, although the three of us were served in a room on our own. The main course was brought in – two sizable stainless-steel cooking trays of liver and onions. I happen to like liver and onions but I know I'm in a minority (a minority in our family certainly) so we admired the director's embrace of risk.

But the visit wasn't to finish quite so easily. The director said, 'You have to meet the music teacher and hear her star pupil sing.' By this time we would have agreed to anything (that didn't involve surgery) so we arrived in the Music Room – which had no other pupils in it because school was over for the day. The music teacher sashayed in with the star pupil in tow. After an animated chat with us she gave the star his cue so he could launch into 'that famous English song – "My Bonny Lies Over the Ocean"'.

Rod and I looked at each other with carefully concealed eye-rolls. The star sang the first verse and we wondered if he would go on to the second. It was not to be. As soon as the first verse ended the music teacher rallied us to the cause with, 'Let's all join in singing the chorus!' Punch-drunk on culture, Rod and I eventually staggered back to the hotel.

Not all our visits were so unprepared. Before we left England a friend had given us a contact in Ufa – but said it was a 'long shot'. The shot was so long we didn't even know if it was a man or a woman. Pam and Diane asked an interpreter to join them as they took up the challenge of deciphering and visiting the address in Pushkin Street. The door was opened by a woman, called Alia, who was just as surprised as Pam and Diane, to whom she showed the very best of Bashkir hospitality. She was a librarian and her English was almost on a par with many native English-speakers.

All four women wanted to unravel the mystery that had brought them together. Some years before, Alia had worked as the dialogue director on the Bashkir language edition of the *Jesus Film*. The guy who had worked on the recording had kept her contact details – which is how we found her. Alia was delighted to re-connect on the subject of Jesus and since the script is closely based on the Gospel of Luke the conversation took off. Then an odd thing happened. As Pam and Diane explained the significance of Jesus' death on the behalf of us humans one of the women began to weep, and then another and then all four. That visit, on that first day, cemented a lifelong friendship, centred on who Jesus is. We still hear from Alia – most recently an electronic Easter card this year.

Back at the Hotel Tourist, a gregarious businessman from Yerevan in Armenia wandered into the lounge. He spoke a few languages, but none of ours. That wasn't enough to prevent his sociability. His first chosen task was to explain his religion to us. He was a Zoroastrian. That took a while. We then discovered that he could read German, so we gave him a German Bible which he read out loud to us in reverential, sonorous tones. To our further amazement we realised that he couldn't understand a word of German – he had simply learned how to pronounce it!

From the beginning we wanted to understand the university. As you can imagine, they offered 'Bashkir studies' which was a big attraction for us. Diane met a girl from that department who was so delighted to hear about our interest that she promised, on the spot, 'If my baby is a girl I'm going to call her Diane!' (she was seven months pregnant).

I'd never been in a university where so many students were studying philology and also how many students could speak English without ever having left their city. This contradicted my long-cherished idea that you need to learn a language only in its social context. In the evening we were invited to a 'student party'. Banish any ideas of student parties in which you may have participated. The only music at this party was soft elevator-type music to enhance the conversation which was to take place around a circular table. The only students attending spoke good English. And, although we were so keen to learn, it soon became clear that they were gasping to learn about the West.

A girl with a loud black and white polka dot dress

sat down on my left and, without further ado, asked, 'What did you think of the screen-play of *The Silence of the Lambs*?' I knew right away that I was going to be a disappointment to her, having never read the screenplay, seen the film, or even developed an inclination to research that genre.

Quite unfazed, she moved on to other topics, asking me what we were doing in Ufa anyway. I told her, without actually saying, 'You're an unreached people group.' Then she surprised me again by volunteering that Bashkir people can be open to new things. 'You know, we only accepted Islam fairly recently, around the 13th Century.' 'So what did you believe before that?' I asked. 'Oh, we believed in the great Creator God.' I think I looked unconvinced, but she charged ahead, 'We still have it in our hearts, and I'll tell you how I know. When my grandmother is knitting and drops a stitch, she calls out "Tengre!" – that's our name for the Creator God.'

You had to be ready for anything. A girl called Yelena walked up to Pam after a lecture and said, without further elaboration, 'Will you teach me to pray?' Cool as a cucumber, as if she did it every day of the week, Pam sat her down in the corridor and taught her essentials of that most basic skill, including the praying of an impromptu demo prayer right on the spot. Yelena said, 'Thank you, can we meet tomorrow so you can teach me more?' They met, they prayed, they learned and then began a long-distance correspondence.

Pam was also in our group that was researching high

culture. Phil, through music contacts, had reached a Bashkir poet who gloried under the name of 'Salawat' (same as that great 17th Century liberator, no less). This modern-day Salawat was blind, much celebrated and invited the group to meet him for a round of discussion. Salawat duly recited his material and then enquired about the group's interests.

Phil realised that the poet was getting a once in a lifetime opportunity and launched forth with an explanation of what motivated the group – gratitude to Jesus Christ for going all the way to give his life for us. Salawat listened intently till the translator finished the whole story and then exclaimed his approval of the Jesus story, 'Wonderful – let's drink to that!' He explained that he was searching for a solid philosophical base for hope, so his art would not be guilty of projecting foolish optimism. Vodka appeared from nowhere and despite the fact that Salawat was blind and that the group included some teetotallers, everybody felt obliged to do the right thing, the Russian way. So that's how Pam drank her first and only alcoholic toast to Jesus.

As we left Ufa airport after that first visit, we made our way through the Intourist lounge once more and happened upon dear Miss Redlips again. She gave Diane a sly wink as if to say, 'Don't worry, you don't owe me five dollars.'

CHAPTER 21

STICK INSECTS AND SUETONIUS

Ufa students' appetite for contact with us 'Jesus followers' was not going to be satisfied by our one visit, so it wasn't long before various ones of us returned to Bashkir State University and some of that original recce group stayed on to live there. Our friend Dr Arthur Williamson from the University of Ulster at Coleraine was invited to come and lecture on Christianity and history. A keen audience heard his explanation that it was simply not good enough to pick and choose the bits you like out of the Gospels' account of Jesus. He quoted C.S. Lewis's comment that if you removed the miraculous bits the rest of it would fall flat. 'You cannot possibly do that with Christianity…It is precisely one great miracle. If you take that away there is nothing specifically Christian left. There may be many admirable human things which Christianity shares with all other systems in the world, but there would be nothing specifically Christian.'[16]

16 C.S. Lewis, "The Grand Miracle" *God in the Dock* (Eerdmans: 1970) 80

I ran into Yelena again – the girl who had asked Pam to teach her to pray the previous year. In the meantime, she had decided to follow Jesus permanently. Her family had let it be known that they were pleased at the positive difference in her life. I asked Yelena how things were going. Her answer, in that oh-so-fresh, newly-learned English was, 'Frankly speaking, I'm doing better every day.'

Because of my science background I was also an object of curiosity, so I got asked to address the issue of Christianity and evidence. What was the evidence for the historicity of Jesus, for the existence of God? What was the connection between natural selection and evolution? As before, I spoke in English and their eloquent questions showed how accurately they understood.

For the talk about dating the earthly life of Jesus I gambled on the suspicion that they would know the lives of the Caesars. So, across a long stage, I set out pictures of the twelve Caesars mentioned by the Roman historian Suetonius – Julius Caesar, Augustus, Tiberias, Caligula, Claudius, Nero, Galba, Otho, Vitellius, Vespasian, Titus, Domitian. Many of the students knew the correct order. This astonished me. I then showed that the death and resurrection of Jesus is dated during the reign of Tiberias (14-37 AD) and before Caligula (37-41 AD).

Now came my gamble. Would they get it if I pointed out that they were accepting the dates 'Anno Domini' without question, thus giving the historicity of Jesus a higher level of authenticity than the Caesars. They got it.

I have never summoned up enough confidence to try this with a Western student audience. Maybe I don't move in the right milieu of young people who have a firm grasp of the Classics and speak crystal clear English.

We withdrew to the canteen for lunch. The university was keen to ensure that they would be paying for my food and that of a student, Leonid, who had been attached to our group as a great translator. The food servers were alerted to who exactly would be the privileged few whose meals were paid for. It gave me a distinctly odd feeling to be singled out in the restaurant but they would have it no other way.

Things were proceeding swimmingly enough, until I held out my plate for the main course. 'How many grams of meat would you like?' asked the lunch lady. I was flustered, never having been asked that in a Western university – and furthermore, I didn't know the answer! 'Fifty grams, or seventy-five or a hundred?' the helpful lady prompted me. 'Ah, fifty is fine,' I answered, as all the images of impoverished Russians suddenly re-formed in my head.

But the answer was wrong! It was fine by the lady, but Leonid gave me his most withering look. I had forgotten that he was supposed to follow my lead. And the students in the queue behind us would feel funny about ordering more meat than the Western guy. You live and learn.

Before I went to Ufa to give the 'Natural Selection' talk I decided it would be enhanced by having a living specimen with which to demonstrate. So I visited the

Zoology department in Birmingham University (where we lived at the time) and asked for a stick insect. They were very understanding and gave me a good big insect, enough leaves to feed it for a couple of weeks and a sturdy plastic box in which to transport it across the 2,500 miles, Aeroflot permitting.

I just don't know a more obviously visible case of natural selection. A stick insect can contrive to make itself look like a leaf and will even produce a 'leaf' which appears to have a bite taken out of it by the beak of a particular South American bird. Our specimen was an instant hit and the audience passed it around from one end to the other. I had once asked the Professor of Genetics in Trinity College Dublin how many mutations it would take to produce such a creature and he said, 'Too many'. I passed that on to them.

I presented the insect in all its glory and claimed that somehow God had a hand in its design – and in our human design too. After all, nobody wants to be told, 'You're a nice person but, deep down, you're just a bag of chemicals.' Most people in that lecture didn't want to be told that either. But one student called Max held out. In the question and answer time he declared that he was going to stick with atheism. I asked him, 'Are you an atheist under all circumstances?' 'Yes.' I proposed a few theoretical circumstances to him but he was going to be an atheist in all of them.

Then I took a broad guess and asked, 'Have you ever been in the Young Pioneers?' 'Yes.' 'Do you ever go on a

Pioneers summer camp in Siberia?' 'Yes.' 'Do you ever take your sleeping mat out of the tent at night and lie on the ground and watch the stars?' 'Yes.' 'Are you an atheist then?' 'No.' I was so proud of Max's courage and honesty in front of all his peers. A real man. Much later they told me that, after some more intellectual thrashing around, Max became an eager advocate for Jesus.

And the stick insect? I handed him over to the amazed staff of the Bashkir University Zoology department who assured me that they would look after him but I also noticed that they had a display cabinet of interesting dead insects and the zoologists were eyeing the spaces available for new entrants.

After these lectures we would move to somebody's flat with whoever wanted to turn up to talk some more. One of those who turned up was an intellectually sharp girl called Lena with penetrating questions. She had run the gamut of this world's spiritual options to find a peaceable life and I wasn't quite sure she had succeeded. She showed interest in Jesus but in our discussions she always ended quiet and hesitant.

Just after I got home, we received an email about Lena from Diane Cowles in Ufa which was enlightening: 'She wanted to make sure that I told you... She actually found a church after you left and prayed to ask Christ into her life at that service. Jesus has turned her life around. I don't know how much she told you, but she has struggled with depression and really has been quite a tortured soul.

'It transpires that not only is she married but had a child. Very tragically, her daughter, Arvin, named after a Tolkien character, died 18 months ago, she was only 14 months old. She'd had the flu and hadn't eaten for over a month when she died. The doctors didn't know what to do. They discovered too late that she had cold sores in her mouth which must have made it too painful for her to eat. Lena says that she has been experiencing Jesus as the gentle shepherd and he has brought much comfort to her heart. Things are still very painful as you will understand.'

Pam and I stared at the email. I was glad we met Lena. We were glad Lena met Jesus. We were glad that Diane had stuck with her. But we were heart-broken for her and all the more so, now that she was thousands of miles away. By now we weren't just theoretically enthralled with central Russia – we had wonderful individuals on our minds and in our hearts.

All that Russian time had now helped to crystallise a new thought in our heads. To address the heart of *British* culture there was somewhere we still hadn't given the attention it deserved – London.

CHAPTER 22

LONDON-CENTRIC

Although we hadn't exhausted all the delights of Birmingham, we moved to London which, the locals informed us, was the centre of the universe. There you have a simple choice: live out of town somewhere and pay in the form of transport hassle *or* in the form of rent in the centre of town and be at work shortly after you wake up. We chose the latter.

Raymond Seitz, a recent US ambassador to the UK, had said, 'London is the omnipotent, all-knowing, unassailable hub of the nation, and today's Decision-Making Zone remains an intensely capital-city phenomenon…the national apparatus is concentrated in a few streets that run along the north side of the Thames.'[17] It seemed to us that this was enough reason in itself to commit to making Jesus well-known in 'all the right circles' of that national apparatus.

Soon Pam and I were introduced to one of those communities you only find in national capitals – ambassadors. The person who did that introduction was Katherine Grainger, the wife of a civil servant who

17 Raymond Seitz, Over Here, London, 1998, 115

worked in the Foreign and Commonwealth Office. She was the one who taught us all we know about care for ambassadors. I say 'care for' because, although they are known for their bilateral political and commercial work, they are also human beings, often with unusual stress on their family. They are commissioned to pursue an occupation which is often a solitary one because they cannot easily fraternise with compatriots, for fear of showing favouritism to this or that faction.

Katherine explained to me carefully, just like a good schoolteacher, 'Most everybody who asks for a courtesy visit to an ambassador wants something and ambassadors are trained to detect this. Here's how it works in London: a visitor has 15 minutes, which needs to include an exchange of pleasantries and a succinct introduction of whatever it is they are looking for.' And what happened after 15 minutes? 'The ambassador does a diplomatic cough after 15 minutes if he or she has had enough of you. Of course, they would never say it like this!' And what does the visitor do? 'The visitor knows these rules and makes sure they have their handbag or briefcase closed again at the tenth minute so they can prepare for a graceful withdrawal at the fifteenth.'

I figured that this would weed out many a visitor. But Katherine continued, 'And of course, in our case, there are a couple of other things we need to insert into the 15 minutes – we need to convince them that we aren't on the make to get something out of them, *and* we want to make mention of Jesus on the first occasion.'

This sounded like a nightmare of a relationship scenario to me, but Katherine serenely assured me not to worry, everything would work out OK. Next, she marched me off to join her on one of these appointments. We were to visit an African country's High Commissioner (which is what the diplomatic corps call an ambassador from a Commonwealth country). We did the exchange of pleasantries. Indeed, the High Commissioner was exceedingly pleasant and chatted away making me feel completely at home, talking about shared interests that we had. Furthermore, it transpired that he was a disciple of Jesus, which made that part of the conversation simpler. He was so good at chatting that I lost track of the time, and eventually Katherine discreetly brought our conversation to an end. I noted that we had been there around 40 minutes.

'I thought that was supposed to be 15 minutes?' I asked her as we turned around the street corner to get a bit of privacy in order to debrief the event. 'I know,' she said, 'But the 15-minute rule is only for when they have had enough of you. This time he wanted to talk.' To this day I suspect that Katherine may have even conspired with the High Commissioner ahead of time to give me an easy first experience. And of course, this informal-sounding chatting business is precisely what ambassadors are supposed to be good at anyway.

Not every introduction was so simple. I got a message one day to ask if I could be available to go and visit the North Korean ambassador at short notice – that same week. I agreed and went along accompanied by a Korean friend who could also help with translation. I needn't have worried because the ambassador had also supplied a translator, but at least everyone now knew what everyone else was saying!

We did the introductions (check), then the pleasantries (check), then came the search for shared interests. Much to my amazement we had some, considering that their country is an atheistic state, far away in culture and geography! The embassy translator knew a Swiss friend of mine who had worked out ways to share goat husbandry ideas with mountain farmers in North Korea. (Like they say, you couldn't make it up in a book).

Next, the ambassador asked about what motivated me and I said, 'I am a devotee of Jesus of Nazareth and I aspire to be like him, as he said of himself, "I did not come to be served but to serve, and to give my life as a ransom for many." ' We talked about ransoms and how they work, like in hijacked planes when a ransom is demanded. Sometimes the hijackers want money but sometimes they want an accomplice to be set free. I explained that this was Jesus' plan – he would give his life so I could go free. It had come down to him or me.

The ambassador mulled this over and said, 'Some acquaintances are old but never become friends. Some are new and will be friends forever. You are in the second category.' Maybe he said the same to all his visitors, but of course we had already connected over the goats! As our chat lengthened, I'm glad to say the ambassador broke any imagined 15-minute limit.

Although we sometimes organised events that we thought would be of interest to ambassadors, they were never on the scale of the embassies' own events. Somehow Pam and I got on the invitation list of a clutch of embassies and were invited to events for their national day, their independence day, their new year, their most famous musician's visit – any old excuse to show off that country.

We treasured those invitations as expressions of trust in us for the simple reason that, in us, they knew what they were getting – people who would talk about Jesus. That, of course, had been made clear at that first appointment. It put us on our mettle to be gentle and respectful with those we met from every continent and faith background.

Bill, an old comrade from the US, joined me in attending a reception given by a strong Middle Eastern country. It was just after the 2004 US Presidential election and many of the attendees crowded around Bill to hear the latest from America. Since we operated a completely non-party policy I wondered how he would field the questions so I loaded up one or two canapés and sneaked over to his corner. He had his conversation partners beguiled with stories of the office plans of members of congress – how poor the facilities were for newcomers and how the old-timers had offices with windows. They found this more interesting than any discussion about who won the actual election. Maybe it resonated because they were wondering what kind of office they would get upon return home – and in some cases, whether they would get one at all.

In a diplomatic world that was still quite male-dominated Katherine surprised us by claiming that it was 'easier for a woman to connect'. That was logical with a woman ambassador but how would it apply for a man she was relating to? In those cases she worked extra hard to get to know his wife. When we ran events for ambassadors it was a constant struggle to find out if the husband was actually going to show up. We would, of course, phone his secretary or the person who ran his diary, but Katherine often had one more trick up her sleeve. She would simply phone the residence the night before and ask the wife (by now, her pal), 'Is he coming tomorrow or not?'!

After a couple of years, Katherine did not always attend such events because she had been diagnosed with a serious cancer. That news was devastating for her, for her family and for us, her friends. If she were here today (and she isn't) I know she would say that only God could have given her an additional eight years to serve him after that diagnosis.

Sometimes Katherine needed treatment in St Mary's Hospital in Marylebone. On one of those occasions, after she had been there for some days, one of the staff asked her, ever so quietly, 'How come you've been here scarcely a week and six full ambassadors have been to visit you?'

(You can't miss ambassadors because their drivers are parked strategically near the front door).

Now we began to see, as never before, how Katherine could love people earnestly. Many in the diplomatic community realised she was seriously ill, although she didn't make a big deal about it. But it seemed like everybody knew. At the last embassy 'do' I attended with her she espied an elegant lady of her acquaintance who was the ambassador from a country of majority Muslim persuasion. Katherine had heard that the lady had troubles of her own and informed me, 'That woman has lost a child in a dreadful accident.' Apparently, the death was so recent that it was one of those cases where you cast around in your mind as to what to say. Not so Katherine, who beetled right over to her and said something which caused them both to cry and hug.

'So how was it?' I said afterwards, 'What did you say?' 'I asked her if she had been able to embrace Christ in her grief.' 'But isn't she a Muslim?' I enquired. 'Doesn't matter – we're all the same. She needs Christ same as I do.' On this occasion there had been no fancy preliminaries because it was now a deep chat between two hurting hearts.

There was much to learn from our diplomat friends – like their unerring instinct for finding common ground. One of them taught me a lot about prayer. I had gone to visit him because his home country was about to have a turbulent presidential election and I offered to pray with him. His country was deeply divided and the news on the ground was that trouble could ensue. We chatted amiably and he readily took to my suggestion of praying.

My idea had been that I would do the praying. I would sit in my chair and he would sit in his. But, quick as a flash, as if it were the most normal thing in the world, he swivelled around out of his chair on to the floor beside his desk and poured out his heart to God about the divisions in his country, the need for peace, the need for reconciliation and the specific personal needs of individuals on both sides of the election. By now I was doubting whether I would even have any contribution to make, but I did. I got to say just one word, 'Amen', when he was done. That almost startled him because it appeared that he had forgotten me. It was the equivalent of dancing like nobody's watching.

Before we left London our little team found a way to do something to help ambassadors, because we had found there was a particular type of connection most of them were looking for – business contacts. We were furthermore delighted to find the 'dream ticket' of a speaker, Ram Gidoomal, a successful and innovative business leader who went on to be a candidate for Mayor of London. He had even written a book on 'The British and How to Deal with Them'. Thirty-seven heads of mission turned up to the lunch at the Royal Garden Hotel in Kensington on the day and took notes as Ram gave his tips.

Ram introduced himself, 'I come from a Hindu family, was brought up in the Sikh faith and was educated at the Aga Khan Muslim school in Mombasa. I became a follower of Jesus in a pub in South Kensington, when I was a student, after a group sang, "Put your hand in the hand of the man from Galilee". A member of the band befriended me and as we talked over a couple of weeks, I found out that Jesus wasn't the man in a bowler hat and pin-stripe suit of my imagination.'

We had invited a good sprinkling of business people so by the end of the morning they were exchanging business cards in a blind frenzy. We also offered the diplomats a copy of the Bible in the language of their choice, which we would later deliver. Twenty of them put in a request for one.

Somehow, I had never thought of business people as being Christian agents although, given the amount of material in the Bible on fair dealing, you'd imagine that would be natural. One person who *had* thought of it was my friend Ed Holtz, whose easy-going demeanour made him a regular feature in the 'City of London' financial district. Ed had started with Agapé in student counselling many years before and now ended up as a mentor to guys who wanted to follow Jesus in the midst of that great machine which is financial London. He claimed that he did this by playing golf really badly. Maybe. Maybe the jostling, aspiring finance guys whom he played with found that comforting. As far as religion goes, Ed maintained he was 'no better than a fringe Anglican'. Again, who could compete with that?

One of these intrepid City guys (and they were almost

all guys) was the director of risk in a national bank. He worked out a way they could meet up for a coaching session on how to be vocal about their faith while at work. Coaching at lunchtime wasn't possible simply because many of them worked straight through lunch which they ate out of lonely Tupperware boxes at their desks. So instead, they met before any of them started work, in an office in the City, early in the morning. One of their venues was Marks and Spencer.

This took the fancy of the *Daily Telegraph* (however they got to hear of it) who wrote, 'Staff at Marks and Spencer are turning to God for help. Employees at the ailing retailer's London HQ have brought in Agapé – a Christian missionary organisation – to help them learn how to spread the gospel. "I have learned to put my points across in a short time," explains one IT worker. "I was even able to explain the basics of Christianity to a work colleague over a sandwich." '[18] At the very least they had a more sociable lunch than normal! It suddenly gave people a licence for a talk that had been for so long pent up, about their souls – soul-talk at work. I'm not sure it helped Marks and Spencer's business, which was never the objective anyway!

What's definitely *not* good for business is bombs. Seven months after we came to London, a homophobic bomber set off a nail bomb in *The Admiral Duncan* pub in Soho, which was 15 minutes' walk from our flat. Three people were killed and many injured. London held its

---

18 Daily Telegraph, April 7, 2001

breath. It was the third such bomb in two weeks. Within twenty-four hours the police apprehended the prime suspect (who was later convicted).

The carnage and the circumstances were harrowing and sobering. Exactly one week after the bomb, the Soho community held a time to pray and reflect in the garden of a church there. One of our team, Brian Weaver, and I went down to pay our respects and give whatever comfort we could to the people in the emergency services who had gone above and beyond the call of duty. These included a civil servant, police officers and a professor of psychology who was heading up the trauma counselling.

After the respectful time in the garden we moved into a room in the parish centre to chat. In the light of all that had gone on it was eerily quiet and courteous. The civil servant regaled me with half his life-story. He had studied spiritual ideas in various institutions around London and concluded that 'it's not good enough to say that Jesus is just a good teacher – he has to be the Son of God,' My gobsmacked self agreed and we talked. 'I know that is a decision I have to make for myself,' he told me.

The senior police officer, who had also moved in from the garden, chatted cordially and told me about his experience of the bombing, which was now just seven days ago, as if it were in history. He informed me that the Metropolitan Police used 'sector policing' in Soho – meaning that police are deployed all across the area all the time. They get to know the area and its inhabitants very well. And when there's a crisis, nobody needs to 'call for the police' – they're already there, with enough first aid skills to save a life. He described kneeling down on the pavement helping people injured by the bomb, vaguely conscious that someone was kneeling beside him handing him equipment and various articles he required as he tended to the wounds. When the work slackened he looked up to see who his helper was – only to recognise that it was a less-than-legal local prostitute. It was that kind of a day.

And that kind of day made us *want* to give our time 100% to Londoners – but by now we felt pulled in two directions. The other direction was the old friends living in Ufa, and new friends there too. It felt like we couldn't help a personal bias towards the Russian friends.

CHAPTER 23

LENIN'S LEGACY

Our original 'motley crew' took a hard look at the map of Russian demographics and decided we'd like to know how Jesus could be introduced to the Tatar people of the Russian Republic of Tatarstan. Some of our team had visited the previous year and the university enticed us back by telling us all we had to do was get to Moscow. Then, our train travel to the capital, Kazan, our accommodation, and special course of study in Tatar language and culture would be provided by the V.I. Lenin University. Lenin *did* study there – but only for three months before he was expelled for doing typical Lenin things.

Kazan's relationship with the Kremlin in Moscow has been, to say the least, testy, because there is an uncomfortable relationship between the two. The Kremlin is famous for its commanding St Basil's Cathedral with its onion dome roofs. But not every postcard tells the whole story that St Basil's onion domes were intended to commemorate the Russians' conquest over the Tatars by the forces of Ivan the Terrible. And the even trickier part of the story is that Ivan's Russians portrayed themselves as 'Christians' while almost all of the Tatars were (and still are) 'Muslims'.

Nowadays there are Tatars living all over Russia. Many taxi drivers in Moscow are Tatars. I get an odd sort of satisfaction, on their behalf, out of the fact that they make money by ferrying tourists to see the Kremlin with its onion domes.

That's why, in March 1997, we ended up in Moscow all over again. And the V.I. Lenin university was true to its word. The train journey to Kazan was like a film set. The view out the window was mostly forest, stretching as far as the eye could see. We were blessed with that magical mix of winter night weather – clear sharp air, no streetlights and snow.

The train was in no hurry – it took us 20 hours – so we got to see numerous stopping points en route, where locals came to sell their wares in the middle of the night. There was a strange poignancy in being offered crystal chandeliers for sale at two in the morning by the men who made them. The glass glistened along with everything else. The men's only problem was that they hadn't been paid at their factory for three months and now had to resort to direct sales. Rod went out and talked with them. The rest of us pressed our noses against the chilly windows to see if there was any transaction taking place. I was lost for a moment in the fantasy of arriving in Tatarstan in style with a chandelier. But no, Rod gave them earnest encouragement, like a half-time pep-talk.

Nothing was sold.

Daylight dawned as we arrived in Kazan, and we temporarily forgot the majestic forest, because there on the train platform was the university's Head of International Relations. His first words were, 'Can you believe it?! Chelsea won on Saturday night!' Thankfully Andy, on our team, had done his homework and had brought him the gift of a football, which he clasped like it was a treasured possession from Britain (although there's a high percentage chance that any such football would be made in Pakistan).

We weren't in language classes all day (although sometimes it felt like it) and the university was a good social gate into the city. We discovered little groups of students who sometimes were more spiritually perceptive than those in other parts of Russia. We put it down to the distinctive mix of origins still swirling around in the cultural whirlpool. In one such group of students a girl announced, in front of her friends, 'The aim of my life is to find my God. There can't be a "Christian" god, a "Buddhist" god and a "Muslim" god. There can only be one God and my life's goal is to find him.' I found this an extraordinary declaration to make in front of her classmates.

Another student, called Marat, took me out to coffee and, after a long discourse on Russian history, quite suddenly said, 'I embraced Islam five years ago but I want to know what it means that if we accept the sacrifice of Jesus' blood we can be born again.' His vocabulary and his formulations were cast in such Christian terms I felt alerted that all this was streaming from some other source. I had to ask him where he got all these ideas, since this wasn't normal parlance in Kazan student street café society. He explained that it *was* a student, a language student from Scandinavia, whom he had met a few semesters previously, who had introduced him to the idea of Jesus as a sacrifice.

Before long I would be in the thick of the same discussion but at a more intense level. Indirectly, through Marat, I was invited to talk to a class of Turkish teacher training students in Kazan. That's not as exotic as it may sound. The Tatars and their language are, like the Turks, 'Turkic'. Thus Turkey had a keen interest in helping Tatarstan, which stretched to the Turkish government financing a cadre of teachers to go up to Kazan and help out. The word had got out in student circles that I was involved in 'both science and religion'. This sounded to the Turks like a strange bird. The word on the street (their street, anyway) had been that scientific and spiritual interests were at odds, if not fisticuffs, with each other.

The Turkish training supervisor happily announced to his class (and me) how interesting and harmonious my talk would be. No pressure there, then! I was to talk about 'Why belief in God and the study of the natural world actually assist each other.' 'You'll find out that what Muslims and Christians believe about God is exactly the same!' he beamed. 'Oh no, you won't,' I reminded him. Then other students joined in the cheery pantomime response, 'Oh yes, you will! 'We are on the same path,' the head man assured me.

I put it to the group to watch the path of my argument carefully as I lectured and to see how quickly they could detect the fork in the road. They signed up to this idea and I made a mental note that maybe I should do this with all audiences, so keen were they to follow my logic. We made our way through the natural world – from cosmology to microbiology looking for evidence for the existence of God.

We then launched forth into the evidence from God's self-revelation – the students were still with me. Then God revealing himself in Jesus – still OK. The supervisor looked at me as if to say, 'See?!' I traced some details of the life of Christ – everybody was still hanging on. But the fork in the road was about to arrive with the crucifixion, about which there are so many well-attested eye-witness accounts. The Turks seemed almost sad to part intellectual company with me – Muslims believe a range of options to avoid the death of Jesus. When I eventually left, we were on good terms, still believing differently but doggedly determined to respect each other.

Only when I returned home did I find why some of our Kazan discussions had been intense. I discovered that Tatars across the world had their own email chat-page (in English!) where they explained their fascination with Christian missions. One said that this interest was being shown by Christians because of 'the weariness of the newly independent or autonomous Muslim states such as Tatarstan where communism's secular and anti-Islamic teachings are still prevalent'. That was a fair comment. I hoped too that an open atmosphere like that of the Turkish teacher training college would prevail.

After some of our permanent team, who had lived in the city of Ufa, later moved to Moscow they suggested we come and see a different kind of university there, where 10,000 students from over 100 countries had converged. In the Khrushchev era the idea had struck somebody to set up a university that would give an advantage to students from countries which had yet to decide on which side of the Cold War they would end up. This hearts and minds campaign was eventually to be called the 'Peoples' Friendship University of Russia' and because it attracted students so broadly, you could meet people from just about anywhere.

Pam and I flew out from Heathrow to join with another group of assorted friends to visit this new (to us) Russian university with yet more introductory language classes. This institution indeed was different. We compared notes at the end of our time and found we had met students from Chechnya, Afghanistan, Guinea-Bissau, Zaire (now Congo), Brazil, Jamaica, Kazakhstan, Armenia, a girl from Guatemala who somebody met on the running track and a Bangladeshi guy from the UK.

We were assigned a young energetic language teacher whose philosophy was to get to know us students through questioning us in English first before then jumping into basic Russian. She went around the room, came to Pam and me, and picked me for the gentle interrogation. 'Do you have a family?'

'Yes.'

'Boys or girls?'

'Two boys.'

'What do they do?'

'One's a rapper and the other is selling ice-cream in San Francisco Zoo.' At this, her eyes widened.

'Do you have brothers and sisters?'

'One of each.'

'And what do they do?'

'My sister is a missionary in Africa.' This she considered as almost impossibly exotic. I'm sure visions of big game were going through her head. Now I think she was breathing faster at the anticipation of what the brother might be doing.

'And your brother?'

I hesitated, because explaining the nuances of my excellent brother's work might be lost on her so I gave a true, somewhat stock answer.

'He's a financial advisor.'

'Boring!' she exploded.

We tore ourselves away from such lovely people after two weeks and flew home through Munich. Munich airport was agog. Each TV monitor was switched to news. It looked to me like a disaster movie showing planes crashing into big buildings. Somebody said it was New York. A big Australian man in front of me was crying. We didn't have quite enough time to work it all out before our London flight was called. Nothing was said about it by the captain or crew, calm as ever. When we landed at Heathrow, we got a call from a team-mate to say, 'The government says London is closed.' 'What do you mean "closed"?' we asked, wondering if this meant all of London, central London or our own district. 'Dunno, that's all it says.'

We made it to the car park to pick up our car. The battery was flat. They say you always remember where you were on September 11th 2001.

CHAPTER 24

FILLING THE EMPTY PLINTH

By the timely efforts of an RAC rescue guy we made it into town. One has to get used to the nomenclature. Londoners call London 'town' as in 'I met Jeremy in town the other day.' However 'City' is reserved for the financial district, 'The City of London' as in 'Gillian has snagged a great job in the City.'

So in our part of 'town' there were 20,000 students living, and 40,000 students studying, within a ten minute walk from our street. Within the Circle Line on the Underground there were 83,000 students. London sustained 60 university institutions. It was not only the greatest concentration of students in Britain, it was also the most diverse in terms of nationality. We were keen to find out how student welfare worked here.

In a lot of places, the first stop would be a university chaplain, so I thought I'd give this a try. The nearest university was University College London so, late one afternoon, I went in search of their chaplain only to find out that they didn't have one. UCL was established in 1826 to serve the intellectual needs of students in England who wanted a university education but weren't prepared for the hoop they would have to jump through if they applied for the only other English options (Oxford or Cambridge) – they would have had to become Anglicans. You can hardly blame them – with all due respect to Anglicanism.

But I wondered if perhaps they had bent their fiercely secular policy a little to tap the potential of a useful chaplain. So I made my way to one of the main university buildings in Gower Street and asked the security man, 'Any idea where I would find the chaplain?' He scratched his head, consulted his long list of phone numbers of their offices but couldn't locate the chaplain. 'That's odd,' he said. 'There's got to be a chaplain, wouldn't you think?' He then sent me to the imposing university Senate House round the corner on Malet Street. Another diligent security man. No chaplain. After all his hard work I hadn't the heart to tell him that his search was doomed by a decision made in the 19th Century.

Experience taught us that UCL wasn't such a secular wilderness after all. One of our London gang, Euan Woolley, used to spend time with me in the Lower Refectory where we met with a wide range of spiritual interest. It didn't completely surprise us when one day a Filipino student told us that he had already heard about the offer that Christ makes to revolutionise a person's life, but he was plagued with procrastination and had done nothing about it. 'What's wrong with now?' asked

Euan. Our Filipino friend found nothing wrong with 'now' and, at Euan's encouragement, bowed his head and did his business with God. Then he asked us, 'I've been wanting to join the local Christian group – do you think it's too late?' Maybe the Lord had begun to work on his procrastination!

At the other end of Malet Street stood the University of London Union (since changed to 'Student Central') where I later found, not a chaplain, but maybe one better. Another of our gang joined me to visit the president of this most enormous of student unions for a getting-to-know-you appointment. He received us punctually and we stated our business clearly. We were working to help foster the social and spiritual welfare of London students. 'How exactly do you do that?' he wanted to know.

I took this as a green light to launch forth into the niceties of the Christian gospel, but I didn't get very far. 'Let me stop you right there,' says he. 'I think there's something you need to know about me.' He certainly had our attention now. 'I'm a Christian – and I suppose that's why I'm here.' He must have seen the blank look on our faces as we took this in, because he went on to explain. 'Here's how it works – I feel like Jesus is in the next office to mine, coughing quietly as if to remind me that he's there. Keeps me on my toes. Funny thing,' he added, 'since I came into this office nobody ever asked me about it until you came today.' I hope we encouraged him and seeing him in operation certainly convinced us that God has his people absolutely everywhere, chaplain or no chaplain.

We also found out that helping students in London meant helping students from over 100 countries. Just another few streets away, in Fitzroy Square, was the Indian YMCA. This amazing establishment is owned, completely, by the YMCA in India. The staff, the General Secretary, the cooks, everybody – is from India. Each succeeding General Secretary is appointed in India and sent to London. It was started for Indians who came to London to study in the 1920s and needed a first place to stay – which is why their clever YMCAs at home bought a building in London for a hostel.

Today there are many engineers, doctors and lawyers who came directly from India to Fitzroy Square as students who remember their time there fondly. We found an easy partnership with the General Secretary, Jacob Abraham, when I went to see him in January 2001. He told me that all the major religious views in India were represented by students in the hostel, including the extreme ones. 'In fact,' said Jacob, 'The most extreme one told me just the other day, "The only reason we can all have a friendly life in the same place is because it's a Christian house" '. The building is arranged with the cafeteria at the front on the ground floor. It's not a public restaurant but I discovered that they can welcome those who would like to eat there. I can testify that the fish curry is to die for – as I mentioned, the cooks are straight from India!

Another partnership which enriched us was the

unexpected arrival of keen Koreans who wanted to overlap with our team. I'm sure that overlap meant hard work for them and it produced some quandaries for us. For example, I had to get used to meeting their team leader, Seung-Ho Yang. Seung-Ho was a well-read scholar who was highly respected in Korea but, when he would run into me on Tottenham Court Road, he would bow. He had worked out that he was slightly younger than me. That's OK in Seoul, where age is properly respected, but it's a bit odd in Central London.

Another of our favourite keen Koreans was Cheol Baek. He had spent some time in Kolkata (Calcutta) but moved on to London because he reckoned the spiritual needs would be greater there. In the end, he lasted in London longer than we did, making his gospel presence felt by carrying a full-sized cross around London Metropolitan University. He reports that he found an office near the BT Tower where he could be strengthened by spending half the night praying. Nobody else was using it at that hour of the day. For all I know, he may have been there when the next Millennium dawned. And dawn it did.

To be totally factual it dawned in the middle of the night. About 11 pm on that 31st December, with a few friends, we made our way towards the Thames which had been rigged up with a set of 2000 pyrotechnic candles on sixteen barges up the river, referred to as the 'Ring of Fire'. At the stroke of midnight, the pulse of light would proceed up the river at the speed of light. 'They'll be able to see it from space,' the excited government informed us. 'You will want to tell your grandchildren.' Our plan was to arrive at the Thames near Waterloo Bridge, via the Strand. Two and a half million people coincidentally came up with a similar plan. We never made it to the river.

We could only conjecture what those lucky people in space saw. From our position, stuck on the Strand, all we ever saw was that 500-year-old Chinese invention – good fireworks. We tottered home by 1 a.m. and found the TV news explaining that the river never did pulse with fire anyway. It was the ultimate millennial damp squib. Those poor space people.

Thankfully, London had more profound ways of marking the turning of that century. In 1999 Westminster City Council had commissioned the sculptor Mark Wallinger to produce a suitable piece to stand on a plinth at Trafalgar Square which had for years stood empty. Historically, the square had four plinths. Three of them carry enormous statues of famous British worthies but the fourth lay empty for many years because they ran out of money before they ran out of worthies. Wallinger obliged by sculpting a life-size statue of Jesus, in a loin cloth, with a crown of thorns made out of barbed wire.

Not everybody liked the statue. The art historian Sir Roy Strong wrote a scathing column about it in the London *Evening Standard* newspaper saying why he thought it was ill-advised. He thought the artist was mistaken because any Trafalgar Square statue should be in keeping with the huge statues of the Roman gods and their chariots that swirl around the tops of the surrounding buildings.

Richard Chartres, bishop of London, saw things otherwise and quickly penned a letter to the editor of the *Standard* pointing out that Sir Roy had missed the point because 'Jesus came to be exactly our size.'

I was so delighted with his letter that I phoned the Bishop's office right away and made an appointment to see him. As I waited in an outer room, I perused the reading material there – it was a bit like the dentist's. The main leaflet on offer was about Jesus and commemorating him in the year 2000 and beyond. I read it cover to cover. When the bishop arrived, I told him I had read his letter to the newspaper and said, 'You need to know that your attitude helps me get up in the morning.'

He thanked me and deflected the discussion to less probing issues. I took the occasion to ask him about the leaflet too. 'I notice this leaflet says a lot about Jesus but doesn't specifically mention the Church of England. Why not?' 'That day has passed,' the bishop said. He had concluded what many had surmised – that spiritual interest was drifting away from hierarchical structures to some new centres of gravity which were now emerging out of London's mist. Centres of gravity like the arts.

CHAPTER 25

THE WRONG EXHIBITION

Pam and I have always had helpful interpreters of the arts in our son Joel and his wife Danielle. We learned a lot from them that we could transfer to London life. From when Joel was a little kid of around five years old he always said, 'I am an artist,' when visitors asked him, 'What do you want to be when you grow up?' Well, he grew up and he's still an artist – a film-maker, a rapper, writer and designer. His media studies degree dissertation was a cultural and philosophical study of hip-hop in the 1990s. Shortly thereafter he left for the US to join a travelling rap group, Dead Poet Society.

After 18 months of honing his skills, he returned to Birmingham to be an Agapé youth worker with secondary school students. His rap background fitted right in. As well as running rap workshops at various schools, he also organised Cypher, an annual get-together of UK Christian rappers, DJs and breakers. The Big Issue review said,

'Any attempt to get 100 hip-hop artists together in

a room sounds like a recipe for a collision of egos and puffa jackets…At first glance, religion and rap are not a marriage made in heaven and about as appropriate as Cliff Richard at a Marilyn Manson gig…

'Joel Wilson claims that rap has its roots in church history. "Rapping takes something from the ecclesiastical tradition in the way that rappers are like preachers. Rap is rhythmic speaking and when certain preachers get going there's very little difference…People think that Christians have cut themselves off from the world when we should be getting our hands dirty." '

Now Pam gets satisfaction out of being known by some good Birmingham rappers – we didn't see that coming!

While in the US, Joel was wise enough to befriend a singer called Danielle. They married in 2000 and soon they were both advising, counselling, coaxing, helping young people who were doing the normal thrashing around, working out what to do with their lives. I remember Danielle telling us, shortly after she was introduced to the young teenage girls she was aiming to help, 'Their entire goal in life is to get to be 16 years old and have a baby!'

Of course, the teenage answer to Danielle would have been, 'What's wrong with that?!' The struggle of many students to construct their system of 'right' and 'wrong' attracted Joel and Danielle's attention and was eventually expressed in an art exhibition for teenagers which they devised 'to contemplate the issue of wrong in society or in themselves'.

Their manifesto was clear: 'We believe that art is a vital part of life, not just an optional pursuit. We want to express our creativity and faith, not only by demonstrating worship to God through our art forms, but also by telling others our spiritual stories and about our encounters with Jesus, the GodHero…We decided to curate an exhibition in our city that would challenge people, young and old, to confront wrong, instead of tiptoe around it or ignore it altogether.'

They wrote to ten schools within a five-mile radius – somehow, eleven responded! They proposed to supplement the work of art teachers 'by offering a chance for young artists (aged 14-18) to create a piece of fine art inspired by questions like these:

'Is war wrong?

Is murder wrong?

Is the term "wrong" wrong?

How do you measure morality?

Does evil exist?

Is lying under oath wrong?

Is racism wrong?

Is revenge wrong?

Is country music wrong?

If there are no absolutes how can anything be absolutely wrong?

Is illicit drug use wrong?

Is greed wrong?

What is wrong?'

In the end, two hundred students would produce pieces for the project. After a number of school exhibitions, the strongest pieces from each school went on display at the main exhibition space at the Custard Factory in Birmingham. There was an opening night party and awards ceremony, after which the show was open to the public.

To increase the prestige of the project for young artists, Joel and Danielle also invited established local, national and international artists to interpret the same assignment. Before any school student got as far as the exhibition space, some great artists had already bought into the scheme, including Makoto Fujimura (an award-winning Japanese artist from New York City), Juice 126 (one of the UK's first abstract graffiti artists) and the renowned Irish painter and sculptor Ross Wilson (again, no relation!). The catalogue listed 56 pieces of art –

'Professional artists exhibit their work alongside that of teenagers from 11 South Birmingham secondary schools. Different ages, different media, different world-views, different hurts, different villains. You might be thinking, "Isn't this just one big woe show? A catalogue of negativity?" By no means! It's all about exploring morality and perspectives on wrong without becoming bitter old gits.'

Pam and I made the pilgrimage from London to the Custard Factory and joined the opening night crowd. We were looking forward to seeing the product of aspiring artistic minds and we were not disappointed. One student, Elizabeth Hingley, produced a most striking painting of a fractured image of a girl's face, with a cigarette hanging limply from her lip, entitled Society Pressure on Teenagers to Conform is Wrong.

Danielle created one of the exhibition's interactive highlights. In a smaller room the visitor was faced with a wall of glass jars, each labelled with a vice or 'wrong' thing. To your right sat a big bowl of bright red beans. 'Drop one red bean into the worst jar,' a sign insisted. People took this unexpected moral dilemma seriously, often waiting for others to leave the room before making their selection. But, for me, the masterstroke of the project was its impish title, 'The Wrong Exhibition', allowing those of us with a teenage mind (like me) the deliciously surreal opportunity to make comments to other visitors such as, 'I think you're at the Wrong Exhibition.'

But Joel and Danielle had hit a nerve. They could see that when teenagers (or indeed anybody) looked out of the window in the morning they often thought, 'The world just shouldn't be that way. I don't fit.' That feeling of 'not fitting' was also prevalent amongst people contemplating following Jesus. The narrative in society was that if you're going to follow Jesus you would surely need to get cleaned up first, sand off your sharp, interesting edges and forfeit your personality.

It offended Joel and Danielle that Christian life was misrepresented in this way. Their flat became a haven for those who wanted to get closer to God but felt they might not 'fit' for a host of reasons – like their experience of autism, their sexual orientation, their social inhibitions, their passion for social justice, their generously-gifted artistic flair or their lack of a stable address. Joel and Danielle's daughters became fully accustomed to people piling into their home for gigs, themed parties, music video premieres and storytelling evenings. The flat also hosted a disparate group of Jesus followers who mixed their Bible studies with feasts, balladry, performance art and activism in the hope of acquiring an 'embodied theology.' They ended up meeting in the flat, week after week, for eight years.

As their vision and theology expanded, Danielle decided to pursue a masters degree in Contemporary Missiology with a focus of justice and reconciliation. Around the same time she helped launch the justice movement Red Letter Christians in the UK. Clearly more radical measures were called for, not just to confront the wrongs of the world but also to tear down stubborn cultural barriers that were keeping marginalized people from engaging in church life. So Danielle left her work with Agapé to concentrate on pastoring an inclusive gathering, with a bigger place to meet and with her whole time to give to it. She explained it in a letter to me, 'I am motivated by wanting people to be able to journey with Jesus from wherever they are, even when it's messy and the road isn't always clear.'

Danielle has Joel's full support. Pam says she knows why, 'It reminds me of when Joel went with me to do the shopping on the High Street. I'd turn around and he'd be nowhere to be seen. Eventually I would notice him sitting on the ground talking to a homeless guy outside the Safeway supermarket – not pitying the guy, just talking to him. Which is one of the things that people without homes want most.'

CHAPTER 26

ANGELS AND ARCHANGELS

Not long after we had seen *The Wrong Exhibition*, Pam and I had a growing realisation that in London we too were running into a number of people who worked in media, arts and entertainment, motivated by a Christian commitment. How many, it was hard to tell. They were often quiet types. Even those with performance genes can be all the more introspective off-stage. Like other artists many of them would say, 'I'll let my art speak for me.' After all, that's what art is supposed to do.

I got a glimpse into this world one day when I went to see Frank Dobson MP in his constituency office, not too far from our flat. He was well-regarded locally and I was calling in to pray for him. But while sitting in the office waiting room, I joined another visitor in the normal British weather conversation. She was ahead of me in the queue. One thing led to another in the chat and she told me she was an artist. Then two things happened at once. She found out that I was a Christian and the MP called out that he was ready to see her. 'Don't move!' she whispered, 'I've got to talk to you when I come out. I've just become a Christian and I need all kinds of advice.'

Of course, when she came out, it was my turn. But she waited for me. She told me that God had rescued her from a life overshadowed by what she reckoned was demonic oppression. She had the sensation of, 'Am I the only person in the world who feels like this?' Nothing would satisfy her until I gave her the best contacts I had of like-minded people to meet up with. I suggested a place where a Christian media/arts person hopefully wouldn't feel left out. A week or two went by before I heard from her again. This time it was an email telling me excitedly that she had found the fellowship of people I had recommended. 'The whole experience was very strengthening. Things are looking up. Thank you so very very much for introducing me.'

Even a cursory glance at a tourist map of London showed the imposing front of the National Gallery all along the top side of Trafalgar Square which was marking the year 2000 with a special exhibition entitled 'Seeing Salvation', aiming to show how artists had tried to depict Christ over all the centuries.

I went down to see it the day it opened. It was jammed. I can understand the *Guardian's* reviewer who wrote, 'The exhibition of images of Christ, at the National Gallery, was by far the most popular exhibition in Britain, with more than 5,000 visitors a day...Within a day staff knew they had a phenomenon. People were queueing for hours to get in, moving at a snail's pace because visitors spent so long studying the works.' They quoted the Gallery's director Neil MacGregor's explanation: ' "Seeing Salvation" investigated a theme that has shaped western art through the centuries.'[19]

While I was in the Gallery I bought a book they were selling alongside the exhibition, *Jesus Through the Centuries: His Place in the History of Culture* by Jaroslav Pelikan, professor of history at Yale. I opened at page 1, 'Regardless of what anyone may personally think or believe about him, Jesus of Nazareth has been the dominant figure in the history of Western culture for almost twenty centuries. If it were possible, with some sort of super-magnet, to pull up out of that history every scrap of metal bearing at least a trace of his name, how much would be left? It is from his birth that most of the human race dates its calendars, it is in his name that millions curse and in his name that millions pray.'[20] Couldn't have said it better myself.

It wasn't just the National Gallery. Again and again, we noticed artists of our own era who seemed to be at the forefront of spiritual issues which were leading the country by the nose. An exhibition by Damien Hirst, the doyen of 'Britart', should have given us a clue. It was entitled 'New Religion'. Hirst's idea was that people depend on pharmaceuticals in the same way they used to depend on religion. I went to see his exhibition, at the Tate Modern gallery.

---

19 Guardian, February 10, 2001
20 Jesus Through the Centuries, Jaroslav Pelikan, Yale University Press, 1985

It was called 'Pharmacy' and was set up exactly like a high-street chemist's shop, right down to the bluish fluorescent lights. In the catalogue Hirst says, 'Science seems to be the right one right now...we changed the drug company names to biblical references.' I found the standard of production to be spectacular, as was to be expected of Hirst's work. The other striking aspect was his knowledge of the Bible. Those 'biblical references' in the catalogue weren't just random, but covered the Old and New Testaments, the Passion of Christ and foundational concepts in theology. The point which stuck in my throat was the apparent arrogance of pronouncing that faith in the God of the Bible was open for replacement, at one stroke of Damien Hirst's paintbrush. Sobering. I began to appreciate the scene in which Christian artists worked. They needed to be excellent *and* profound *and* true.

Meanwhile, momentum was building in London among Jesus-followers in the media, arts and entertainment industry, like a subterranean rumble. All they needed was a catalyst to connect them with each other. The resolution came from an unexpected source – Birmingham. Steve Cole was a young music manager there who began to commute to London to join friends across the industry who had shown interest in his three watchwords: humility, unity and prayer. Steve took his time and contacted every conceivable artist who might be interested in praying together. He announced a date and a venue – a building belonging to the Salvation Army on Oxford Street.

Three hundred turned up, mostly amazed that each other existed. One of them said, 'Let's start as we mean to go on – standing at the foot of the cross – this is where we belong.' He then walked over into a dark corner of the building and produced the biggest wooden cross you ever saw. They called themselves 'Artisan Initiatives' and began to meet every month. The 'humility' idea was critical since these were workers in an industry where self-promotion was part of daily life. The monthly pray-ers comprised brand-name musicians, no-name actors and everything in-between, including the slightly anxious performers who, for most of the month were waiting on tables while also waiting for their next job.

Steve's idea was 'nobody leaves here un-prayed-for' and to accomplish this he organised us into little groups of three or four at the end of each evening so we could share personal needs that the others in the group could pray for. I ended up in a group of three one evening with a man (of some artistic streak) and a stylishly dressed woman who hadn't been before – a cut above the normal, for that audience anyway. I shared my little story, the other guy shared his, and then it was the woman's turn. 'Would you mind awfully,' she began, 'if, instead of asking for something personal, I ask for something worldwide.' 'Go ahead, absolutely, be our guest,' the two of us said, wondering what was to come.

'Well,' said Ms Worldwide, 'I want us to pray for a conference in Monterey, in California, where leaders in various fields are going to meet to discuss the future of the world. Al Gore will be there.' Us two guys looked at each other. Now it was time to pray. The other guy chickened out on the Monterey option and did all *his* praying for *me*. Then silence. I prayed briefly for the guy and then said to our new lady friend, 'You know all about the conference, so we think you'd be the best person to pray for it.' She seemed delighted. 'Do you really think so?' she asked. 'Sure, go ahead.'

There followed a remarkable prayer which went like this: 'Dear God, please send an angel to help these leaders to talk together. Or, if possible, an archangel. Amen.' I checked later. The conference was one of the very first TED talks. And Al Gore *was* there.

On the way home on the No. 27 bus along Marylebone Road, I imagined a conversation between the archangel Michael and the archangel Gabriel, 'It looks like one of us is going to Monterey this evening. It's in California.'

There was no getting away from it. Just by locating in central London, Pam and I were now working and living in an art hub. Even the district we lived in was known as 'Fitzrovia', just because Dylan Thomas, George Orwell and Augustus John had allegedly drunk in the Fitzroy Tavern once upon a time. And the playwright Brendan Behan had sung in it!

CHAPTER 27

PASSION FITZROVIA

Fitrovia is a rough square bounded by Oxford Street to Euston Road and Tottenham Court Road to Great Portland Street. The part of Fitzrovia where we lived, at 100 Whitfield Street, was in the Borough of Camden and one day I phoned up the Camden Town Hall with a query. I don't remember what the query was, but I do remember that I was put on hold with music and then realised it was traditional Irish music. 'How appropriate and clever!' I thought. 'By what kind of sophisticated tracking system do they know that I'm Irish! This technological world is a wonderful place.'

But as I kept on holding, the next thing I knew I was listening to bhangra, then after a while it switched to full-on reggae. London is home to so many kinds of people that Camden wanted to celebrate us all! I had coincidentally phoned during the Irish section of the long loop. It started me thinking. Every enthusiasm was getting celebrated.

By this time we also noticed that all manner of people who lived or worked in Fitzrovia shared an enthusiasm for

Jesus. In a back-of-the-envelope calculation we counted about 40 of them who were known to us personally. We would smile and nod to each other in the street. I even discovered a thriving little Chinese church meeting in a house down a lane, five minutes' walk from our home.

Then some of us began to discuss the fact that our square mile was no ordinary context. Commercial enterprises used this area of London to test publicity pitches to markets geographically far beyond it, because of the publicity-sensitive nature of the workforce in this district. Many of the world's top advertising agencies were located in just a few streets around us.

Something appeared to be happening every day – it felt like London had invented FOMO (the fear of missing out). A whale swam up the Thames as far as Westminster one day. There was nothing special about the disoriented whale but it became national news because it poked its nose into Central London.

Pam and I were somewhat bemused when a photographer called Jennie Green turned up at our flat one day explaining, 'I am taking pictures of the buildings on this street to assemble into a special pictorial portfolio of Fitzrovia.' That much was clear, but then she added, 'I am photographing the *inside* of each building and in every case the *resident* needs to be in picture.' It sounded arty, clever and totally odd, all at the same time, but I thought, 'Why not? This is never going to happen again' (you get like this after living in Fitzrovia for a while).

Jennie selected a chair and placed me in the middle

of the lounge facing away from the window and facing her camera, which was an enormous affair behind which she would disappear while setting up the shot. I'd never before been photographed 24 times in a row. She would shoot, I'd hear the click and her head would appear above the parapet again. After maybe the tenth shot she began asking me a question each time she surfaced, starting with, 'Why do you live here?' 'Because this is where the movers and shakers are supposed to concentrate.'

Next question: 'What is your work?' 'I am a national organiser for the following of Jesus of Nazareth.' Long silence. 'How did you get into that?' 'Years ago – when I realised I needed badly to be forgiven and Jesus was offering that.' Shot, click and now a really profound question: 'Do you ever wonder what your life would be like without Jesus of Nazareth?' 'That's easy – just ask my wife here. She'll tell you. I would be a self-centred so-and-so.' She re-surfaced, slowly this time. Soon the photoshoot ended but the chat continued and we promised to keep in touch.

So, our back-of the-envelope group of local friends began to think, 'What effect would it have if we all "came out" as followers of Jesus at the same time?' The answer to the next question, 'When would we do it?' was easy – Easter. After all, people expect Christians to do *something* at Easter time. A wise Anglican minister cautioned us against actually using the word 'Easter' in our campaign because we'd have to waste time re-adjusting the public's ideas about chocolate eggs, bunnies and fertility rites.

'Why not call it "Passion" '? he asked. So our ad hoc group's clever secretary, Brian Weaver, recorded: 'Jesus' passion could very well be a topic of conversation around water coolers, coffee shops, and kitchen tables.'

And so it was that a diverse group of devotees of Jesus of Nazareth called themselves 'Passion Fitzrovia' during April 2004. Others appeared out of thin air as soon as we got started. Some worked in Fitzrovia and had come from other places – New York, Bristol, Northern Ireland, Bath, Japan. Many of them were artists who worked on pieces of art that expressed their feelings about the Passion of Christ. Some brought 'Passion' art to us that they had already produced. All kinds of art. We were covered with art. We were also accumulating art historians – we already had three good ones.

The notion that we could find a single place to exhibit all the artwork was quickly dispelled. We would have to exhibit it 'everywhere', in public spaces all around Fitzrovia which were accessible to the public but secure enough to prevent theft. I was given a list of potential sites to go and scout out, and interview those who owned them.

My first visit was to the Holiday Inn hotel on Carburton Street. I had never done the like before, and I don't think they had either. I talked to the guy at the desk and he asked me to wait for the manager, Nick Campbell, who turned up quite promptly. After I gave a hastily cobbled together explanation of what we were looking for he said, 'Sure. Let's hang them all across the walls of first floor for the Easter season. Would that be alright? I can get the pictures that are currently hanging there moved to storage. Would £100 be sufficient?'

Now I was truly out of my depth. It all sounded very accommodating but what was the £100 about? Was that their rental charge? Maybe he heard me fumbling around looking for words but he explained that the £100 was what *they* would pay *us* for the privilege!

The next stop was the building on Grafton Way belonging to the Venezuelan Embassy. They are rightly proud of that building and its grand 'Bolivar Hall' event space. Simón Bolivar (who helped establish Venezuela – and indeed half of South America) used this house as his London base in the 19th century.

I asked the cultural attaché if we could place some art there. He agreed and knew so much about art that he soon lost me in the conversation. It was all I could do to slow him in his tracks so I could interject, 'You see *I'm* not the artist we're talking about here. I'm just looking for the space for these *other* artists during the Passion season.' Undaunted, he charged ahead and said, 'Where are you holding the opening night?' I had no idea and no plan. 'Why not hold it here!' he beamed. Since no other embassy had offered, they got the gig!

Other exhibition venues followed, like the Indian YMCA, the Clubhouse in Cleveland Street, St Charles Borromeo in Ogle Street, the 'Hope' pub in Whitfield Street and All Souls church beside the BBC in Langham Place.

I should hasten to add that not all the art was pictures you hang on the wall. For starters, we needed someone to design a striking logo for the campaign and Angie Moyler, a designer and a friend of the project did a great job. She took an idea that had appeared on anti-Iraq-war placards (which depicted spots of blood) and adapted it.

A proper curator saved the day on the art front. She was Kaori Homma, a Japanese artist whose background was installation art and a very fine form of etching on mulberry paper (which she made herself – from mulberry trees!). She knew a lot about art, Eastern and Western, she loved Jesus and she could be diplomatic about other people's art – exactly the kind of curator we needed.

One form of art I hadn't expected was film, but we discovered that we had amongst us the co-producer of a new film about the Passion. He was Christopher Gawor and his film *Man Dancin'* (directed by Norman Stone), set in gritty gangland warfare, packs a powerful punch about the self-sacrifice of Jesus. The initial charity showing, in aid of the Teenage Cancer Trust, was already scheduled for two months before Passion Fitzrovia, but the producers kindly agreed to show it again at the Clubhouse, as part of our programme.

It seems that films are like the proverbial buses – you wait for one and two come along. I got a message from a friend in Southern California to say that he had just been shown a test screening of *The Passion of the Christ*, a film by Mel Gibson. He suggested I contact the film's PR man,

Paul Lauer, to see if we could procure a showing of it. So I wrote a *very* polite fax saying, 'Could we have a truly win-win scenario where we give the film unparalleled advance publicity in central London and in return we would gain great impetus for our multi-faceted raising of the profile of Jesus?'

I waited for a quick reply, but none came. Little did we know that Mel Gibson was, by that time, up to his neck in controversy about the film – much of it because it portrayed the death of Jesus up close and personal (it was an age 18 certificate film). *The Daily Telegraph* reported that the Pope had requested a copy to check it out. They said that the film had 'provoked a storm in America with Jewish critics demanding changes'… and 'some Catholics have expressed reservations'.[21] Once the dust settled in California I got a message referring us to the film's international distribution office – which happened to be Icon Films in central London scarcely a mile away from us.

I went to see Kate Giles, the person who ran that office, and we sat there, somewhat astonished by each other. Both of us were aiming at the same thing, previously unaware of each other. I don't think it took her long to work out that I was not a media mogul – but she agreed to incorporating the first UK showing of Mel Gibson's film into Passion Fitzrovia. In fact that showing became our opening event.

Having been buoyed up by having a major player on

---

21 Daily Telegraph December 19, 2003.

board, we then hit a wall of practicality – how do you arrange a film première? I scrambled to contact Chris Gawor for advice and at short notice he and Pam and I hunkered down in the Kentucky Fried Chicken on Edgware Road to sort it out. First Chris told us the bad news – there is no such thing as a go-to check list on running a première. You make it up as you go along, in whatever style you like. At that point I had so many embarrassingly basic questions: 'How do we find a cinema? How do we get them to cooperate with us? How do we even get the distributors to send the film to the right cinema?'

Chris had pity on us. We didn't need to call it a 'première' because we weren't inviting the stars of the film – that would be counter-productive if we want to give Jesus the big billing. He also reminded us that things would get simpler if we had a charity ready to receive the proceeds from the 'gala opening night' event. One charity seemed to be a no-brainer – the Red Cross, which was originally started by a young Swiss businessman, Henry Dunant.

Dunant had spent his early twenties encouraging young people in various European countries to dedicate themselves to Christ. Then, on a business visit to Italy, he saw the carnage of war when he came upon the aftermath of the Battle of Solferino in 1859. This was so horrific to him that he formed what we now know as the Red Cross and convened the Geneva Conventions. (He then went bankrupt, lived his life in obscurity, was 'discovered' again almost at the end of his life and was awarded the very first Nobel Peace Prize!)

The Red Cross in London sounded happy enough to partner with Passion Fitzrovia and the *Passion of the Christ* film when I phoned them up. We arranged to see each other in person to settle the details. I went over to their office but when the publicity woman appeared she said, 'I'm terribly sorry to bring you all this way but we can't partner with the film. We can't be seen to be partisan in religious matters.'

My explaining 'but this isn't endorsing a religion – it's about Jesus being on the cross,' didn't seem to help. I referred to the story of Henri Dunant which had nudged us towards contacting them. She was hazy about the organisation's history, so I simply asked, 'Did you ever ask yourself the question "Why is our cross red?" ' Apparently, and amazingly, she hadn't. I guess she had applied for a top job at a well-known charity and hadn't researched their details very thoroughly. We parted amicably – but not before I took the opportunity to fill in the missing details about Monsieur Dunant and the cross.

The solution to finding an alternative charity partner was staring us in the face. There already was a charity caring for homeless people operating in Fitzrovia in which some of our 'Passion' people were volunteering. It's called 'Aslan' (for All Souls Local Action Network). Their big emphasis was on personalising their contact with rough sleepers and the 'hidden homeless' (people you wouldn't actually *see* sleeping rough but still don't have a place to call home – and don't get into government statistics).

One Aslan volunteer told me about how they dealt with some of the excess food made available by Marks and Spencer. 'It's a funny thing,' he said, 'to wake somebody who's sleeping under Waterloo Bridge at half six in the morning to ask them, "Would you like strawberries or raspberries?" ' The volunteers invited rough sleepers to join them at the Clubhouse for a meal on Saturday night. They called them 'guests', served them a great meal (prepared by a chef) and they would maybe watch a film together and chat. Aslan's director at the time, Chris Peacock, later said, 'The treatment of the "hidden homeless" is a disgrace to our nation.'

So it was no problem to switch our money to Aslan. Except we didn't have money yet. We *did* have the cinema, the Odeon on Shaftesbury Avenue. The deal was done by one of our gallant colleagues, Amy Stroud, who bought all the 8pm seats in the cinema for 26th March on my credit card, as arranged. She sold them all again, at a good profit, to likely customers and friends of Fitzrovia. And then she stood outside the cinema in the cold, on the night of the showing, and sold all the returns – again. So there were 'proceeds' after all.

The film lived up to its age 18 rating. There was no missing the message that Christ died for our sins. I was accompanied by another film director that evening who said, after the showing, 'I was so taken with it that I couldn't even see where they used computer graphics – and that's what I do for a living. I was too distracted by the story.'

Since this had been billed as the 'opening night' of Gibson's film, who should turn up after the show but CNN's man in London, Jim Boulden, plus cameraman, to sample the audience's reaction. 'People we talked to seemed to like it,' Boulden reported. His vox pops included, 'I knew that it was going to be a wonderful thing to see, but it really exceeded my expectations'; 'I think I was expecting a bit more kitsch and I think I saw something that was very realistic and very moving'; 'I did like it, but it's a really, really hard one…I'll think about it the whole weekend I think, yeah.'

Boulden swung the camera again and asked me what I thought. 'People who just regularly go to the cinema on a Friday night will come here and be so deeply impacted by the person and the teaching of Jesus.' Of course, this being central London, CNN presented the overall response as 'the reactions of moviegoers in Great Britain', as if we spoke for everybody.

The CNN episode had an unexpected resonance for Pam and me. We hadn't realised that, at that very time, a dear friend of ours, Barbara Newton, was watching CNN while sitting on a couch at home in the Venezuelan jungle where she was a missionary – and heavily pregnant. The CNN report gave her one of those 'It's worth it all!' moments.

A couple of days later we had the official reception to

launch the Passion Fitzrovia project – in the Venezuelan embassy's building of course. We asked everyone we knew to list everyone *they* knew and made a database for invitations. We included 'the great and the good' – politicians and ambassadors and the like. We got nice invitation cards printed. RSVPs began to come in. That's always encouraging.

The next day was *dis*couraging. While working on the invite cards Amy Stroud said to me, kind of by-the-way, 'Is that how you spell Venezuela?' 'Don't do that to me!' I said, thinking she was joking. But then I checked and I had indeed goofed and sent out however many invitations with a mis-spelled embassy. We agreed to tell nobody and only re-print the cards that would go to ambassadors, who mercifully hadn't had theirs yet. To this day there must be pub quizzes in London where they give a surprising answer to, 'How do you spell 'Venezuela'?'

One of the invitees who responded promptly was Nasim Ali, the Mayor of Camden. He had just been elected, at the age of 34, and so had become the UK's youngest mayor as well as the first Bangladeshi mayor. Fitzrovia was in his patch and we were delighted to have him. It wasn't long after we received Mayor Ali's acceptance that we had an ever-so-discreet call from the office of Westminster Borough. Some bright person there had worked out that there is also a corner of Fitzrovia, however small, which is in their borough. 'We were wondering if you were thinking of inviting the

Lord Mayor of Westminster to your exhibition? You've got the address?' Yes, we had the address. And we were equally delighted to invite and welcome Jan Prendergast, the Lord Mayor of Westminster. We now made sure that both mayors appeared in any photos.

By this time, Passion Fitzrovia's advertising had improved because one of the guys in the project, Alex Normanton, was a graphic artist in a major advertising house. He discovered that some of his contacts in the industry had unused advertising space going idle that they were prepared to let Alex use for free. He sourced images of Christ on the cross from Mel Gibson's people and produced beautiful ads featuring the images overlaid with key words describing Christ. This resulted in oversized ads on Oxford Street's official advertising positions: one showing Christ as 'Friend' outside the Vodaphone shop, 'King' outside Marks and Spencer, and 'Saviour' outside a gaming shop.

Now people began to visit the pieces of art in the various locations inside the 70 streets of Fitzrovia. Some artists gamely gave talks explaining their work. One of them was a flautist and sculptress who lived up the street from us and had no particular Christian background. She produced a piece of installation art using all the equipment used in the crucifixion. She said, 'As soon as I heard about this project I began to study Mark's gospel. It took me three months and then I had to gather all these objects such as the nails that Romans would have used.' Her piece was accompanied by the sound of wind chimes and the whole effect was suitably eerie and disconcerting.

We were favoured with some valuable pieces – Tiger Aspect films lent us a painting by the illustrator Charlie Mackesy. But the art that had the most effect on me personally was shown by our curator herself, Kaori Homma. Entitled *Atoned* it was housed in St Charles Borromeo and consisted of a small, heavy cast-iron duck resting on a deep red sheepskin rug.

In her talk to the visiting public Kaori explained that she and her husband Ken McLaughlin had a daughter who, when she was a little girl, had been very ill with a brain haemorrhage, to the point where her life hung in the balance. There was nothing they could do for her and they prayed desperately and earnestly. She saw this as a metaphor of our utter dependence on Christ to rescue any of us. That's why she had dyed the sheepskin red. She had cast the iron duck using the shape of a feather-light plastic bath toy. Although it was now very heavy it was supported by the sheepskin on the floor.

A toy duck, a little girl, a strong red rug and a reminder, to me anyway, that I am also 100% dependent on Christ's sacrifice, right there in the middle of all that art.

By the time we left London four years later, Mayor Ken Livingstone couldn't help remarking in a press conference that church attendance (which we knew wasn't his favourite hobby) had grown over the previous ten years. Some of those new church attendees were artists, some diplomats and a careful statistician had worked out that over 50% of church attendees were not white. That was a lot for Mr Livingstone to take in.

CHAPTER 28

POST-SECULAR

It's funny how Irish people will always forgive you for leaving the country, so long as you come back, no matter how long you were away. In 2008 Pam and I came back from London to a different Ireland from the one we left 22 years before. We were constantly informed that people were now more 'secular', although nobody seemed quite sure what that meant. It seemed to mean that the Catholic church wasn't in control of so many aspects of life. Our next-door neighbour, a hairdresser, told us that she went to Mass whenever she felt she needed a psychological lift. This was supposed to show us that she was still religious, but it had the opposite effect. It showed that she now felt in control of her own destiny for a change.

This 'swing' to 'being secular' was confirmed to me by Mike Nugent, chairperson of Atheist Ireland whom I met at a Trinity College debate after he had excoriated church ministers for abuse and hypocrisy. I assured him, 'You are sounding more like Jesus every day.' 'How so?' he wanted to know. When I told him, 'Jesus reserved his bitterest criticism for the representatives of organised religion,' he seemed pleased. 'Never thought of that!'

Then there was a rush of people trying to renounce their baptism. A website was set up for this purpose so you could even 'de-baptise' online. In the cause of fairness, some Church officials cooperated with this process, but after a while it collapsed because those aspiring to be un-baptised were told that Canon Law would not allow them to leave the Church. The applicants then gave up, since they rated Canon Law to be the last word. At the expense of being rude, I secretly found this hilarious – I thought that Canon Law was precisely the kind of thing from which they were trying to escape as meaningless and now they were kow-towing to it again.

In May 2020 Fintan O'Toole wrote an article in the Irish Times on the occasion of Bono's 60th birthday. O'Toole put the spiritual conundrum like this: 'For a Catholic Ireland that was secularising gradually at first and then very rapidly, Bono's old-time religion is hard to fathom. ... The frame of reference within which Bono's biblical sense of calling might be understood is mostly absent... Bono's big book has always been the Bible.'[22] Whatever you think of Bono, the conclusion rings true – having the Bible as your 'big book' was mostly an absent framework.

The whole secularisation narrative was overlooking a major flaw, best put by the English writer G. K. Chesterton, over 100 years ago: 'When men stop believing in God

22 Irish Times, May 9, 2020.

they don't believe in nothing; they believe in anything.'[23] The issue at stake was not the intricacies of religious hierarchy but who you believe. Newspaper reports revealed, in survey after survey, that when people were asked about their beliefs they instead recorded their membership of some particular denomination system, whether they chose it or whether (as in most cases) somebody else chose it for them.

Another phenomenon you couldn't miss was the growing popularity in Ireland of the Camino de Santiago, a revived, age-old pilgrimage across northern Spain. Few people took on the journey out of a traditional Catholic motivation – mostly it was a more mystical search. It's not unusual to meet a Buddhist or a Muslim on the pilgrimage. Encouraged by an Agapé colleague, Kelly Mulholland, I first walked the route with students from various European countries, with different groups each day. When you walk with somebody for more than a couple of hours you run out of small talk and eventually revert to listening to your walking companion ponder the deeper questions of life.

One day, after our conversation drifted to talk about the historic person of Jesus Christ, one of the students, from Lithuania, told me she had now decided to get right with God at Easter the following year. On the one hand I was happy, but on the other hand I wondered how she would get on in the meantime. Pressurizing her would have been not only non-Christian but also just bad

23 Emile Cammaerts, Chesterton: The Laughing Prophet (1937).

manners. When I went home I began to sneakily enquire of my friends in Vilnius whether the girl had upgraded to an earlier date – which she had!

Soon Kelly moved to Dublin from Spain and had dozens of Irish students, through his Agapé connections, signing up for the Camino every year – mostly those who were about to go to university. Each day the walkers had time to walk, time to reflect and a time to share their thoughts. Those who followed Jesus, and those who didn't, talked about what they had learned. Everything was done slowly.

I got interested, as never before, in what Irish people actually believed. When promoting Jesus is your thing, you also get interested in which other figures are getting promoted as having ultimate claims. But where do seekers look for such new spiritual opportunities? More by accident than design, I stumbled on just such a market. The Royal Dublin Society was hosting the 'Dublin Mind Body Experience', an exhibition which served as a platform for remedies to curious spiritual diseases. As one of the exhibitors, Maren Palm, an artist, put it, 'Art is my key to use to unlock the chambers in my soul, which I didn't know existed.'

The exhibition was soon about to start so I phoned the owner of the 'Dublin Mind Body Experience', Freddie Roberts, and asked if he could provide a space for us to come and present Jesus as a viable option. 'You mean, you're Christians?' he asked. When I confirmed this I could hear him smile on the phone, 'Well, well,

well – now we've got everything covered!' and he quickly jumped to say how welcome we would be.

Freddie rented us a good corner space in the RDS's 'Industrial Hall' and we asked a local printer to print out, across three pop-up banners, 'I am the way, the truth and the life', the famous exclusive claim of Jesus as recorded by John, his friend and disciple. Pam and I phoned around friends in town to see who would like to staff the exhibition stand with us – a stand which had no logo, no brand, no church – just an introduction to Jesus. Twenty such friends turned up across the weekend, representing each age decade, from their 20s to their 70s.

We were interested in both the general public who visited (by the thousand) and our neighbours on the adjacent stands. Gosia, the friendly young woman on the very next stand was 'representing applied biomagnetic therapy'. Pam explained to her that we were representing Jesus. They had good chats over the weekend. Another near neighbour had resurrected the Victorian art of framing one's dead loved-one's hair. On the other side of the exhibition aisle was a list of the places in Ireland where you could get healed and listen to a man who would 'tell you the truth', with the aid of small bottles of variously coloured liquid.

The visitors to the exhibition were just as varied. We listened intently to what they came to find. One of the questions we asked them was, 'Off the top of your head – what do you think was the best thing Jesus ever said?' The front runner, by a long shot, was, 'Love your neighbour as yourself.' Whenever we could do so politely, we pointed out that this statement was not original to Jesus (he was quoting it from the Old Testament of the Bible) but *his* new idea was, 'Love your enemies.' My favourite answer was from a passer-by who thought a long time to come up with his 'best thing Jesus ever said' which was, 'This too shall pass', wherever he got that.

It didn't take us long to see that there was a gap in people's minds where the Bible used to be. However, Jesus was still a good brand, despite the fact that it was based more on a faint rosy memory than on any substantive content. To those who wanted to stay a while and chat we offered a nicely bound copy of the Gospel of John.

When we had packed up our stand after the weekend I got a message from Freddie, the organiser, to say, 'Thanks so much for being a part of the event.' It was a win-win deal. We got to meet and talk with (and sometimes pray with) the curious-minded Irish general public. But our little team went through a massive learning experience to hear, face to face, where the average person is at, spiritually. Our team included a lawyer, three students, senior lecturers in University College Dublin and Dublin Institute of Technology, a financial advisor and a counsellor. *Plus* a Nigerian pastor, John Eniola, who brought something with him that the rest of us didn't naturally have.

John has a world-view that instinctively sees the world around us as a spiritual space, as distinct from our so-called 'Enlightenment' view of a purely mechanistic universe. He could understand the thirst being expressed in the souls of those visitors who graciously gave us their time at the exhibition.

I first met John when he came to visit our Agapé office in Dún Laoghaire. He asked if we could provide him with video copies of the *Jesus Film*. He had worked in television in Nigeria and had found the film useful there. We settled down to talk. One of our team, Chloe Hanan, asked if John would like a cup of tea. His answer, which we have since got to know well, was, 'Two sugars'. John wasn't planning to show the film to fellow-Nigerian friends, as I had imagined. He wanted to show it 'to young Irish men in the streets – in the gutter'.

Then the whole story tumbled out. He had been educated, like so many others in Nigeria, by Irish Catholic priests – through primary and secondary school. When the chance came to work in Ireland he jumped to take it, 'to see if there was anything I could give back'. I had heard this sentiment before from kind Africans who had come to live here, but John's idea was different. He said, 'Ireland is in trouble now but God has given us the answer – it is in young Irish people. Not just me preaching. It is in young Irish men and women who are in the gutter today. God can transform their lives and then they will be the ones to bring the country back to God.' That's why he wanted the *Jesus Film*.

So where did this business of 'the gutter' come in? It wasn't metaphorical. While visiting Dublin from his home in Cavan, John had joined his wife and daughter to eat at a Chinese restaurant in Marlborough Street. On the way in, John noted that there were some people sitting on the pavement – in the gutter. On leaving the restaurant again he said to his daughter, 'Are those the same guys who were there earlier today?' His daughter explained that they were begging for food. 'We've got sandwiches in the car,' John said. Sandwiches which had been destined for use in his church in Cavan soon became popular fare in Marlborough Street. They were all eaten in 30 minutes.

The grateful recipients innocently asked, 'Do you do hot food?' John answered, rather too quickly, 'Aaah, yes,' before he had worked out how on earth he could fulfil such a promise. 'When would you have it?' they wanted to know. 'Aaah, Tuesday.' 'Great! Thanks!' By now the gears were whirring in John's mind, wondering if he could persuade the women of the church in Cavan to make enough portable hot food by Tuesday. Those gallant heroes of the faith came up with the goods which were then provided the following Tuesday out of the back of John's little van, back on the street in Dublin. I don't think John had anticipated the next question on the street, 'Would you do this every Tuesday?'

Which is how John Eniola was catapulted from living a relatively quiet life in Cavan, minding his own business, to spending more and more time with young Irish people 'in the gutter' waiting for God to transform their lives. Not only did his little van attract the attention of the needy, the addicted and the hopeless in Marlborough Street, it came under the vigilant gaze of An Garda Síochána who pointed out to John that it was actually illegal to do what he was doing on a regular basis. Indeed, doing it regularly in the same spot on the street was the problem – he couldn't stay. He would have to move around.

That night, when John went home, he wrote a letter to the Inspector in the Store Street Garda Station, near his regular van-parking spot. In the letter he explained 'Seven Reasons Why' he should deliver free hot food to those who needed it on Tuesdays. One of his reasons was that God himself had impressed on John to do this. This was not a letter to commit to the post. It would be hand delivered. In short order, he returned to Dublin, to Store Street, and secured an appointment with the said Inspector. I can only imagine the Inspector's morning as this very courteous, very passionate, very compassionate man appeared in his office. John went through the seven points, skipping none of them.

When the Garda on the beat appeared the next Tuesday, the van was back, the food was back, the hungry were back – and the resulting traffic jam in the area was back. But there was now a new element, which John showed him. It was a list of seven reasons why the van should be there, now countersigned by the Inspector.

John's centre of gravity was moving to Dublin and all he needed now was a unit in an industrial estate in North Dublin. That was where he began to shepherd a growing flock of his so-called 'gutter' people who had become his friends and whose lives were being visibly transformed into productive and outward-focussed citizens – exactly what John had expected God to do.

Life in this nascent church community took an unexpected turn on Sunday morning, December 6th, 2015 when they had an unexpected visitor – with a balaclava and a sawn-off shotgun – who sneaked into the back of the building. The intruder then gave a bag to a member of the congregation and forced them, at gunpoint, to go around and collect the mobile phones and wallets of the 60 people in the congregation who were now all lying on the ground.

The gunman left as quickly as he arrived and drove off at high speed. It took a few hours for the Garda report to appear in the national news but I knew right away whose church this was. I phoned John the next morning. His reflection on the whole incident was, 'Now I know we came to the right district. This is a place where people need the Lord and so we need to be here.' No talk of backing down, backing out, or moving away. In fact, he realised that some of those whose lives he wanted to touch were beyond his reach – because they were in prison. But not beyond reach for long. John's instinctively direct method of operating led him to the door of Fr Peter McVerry, surely the most respected priest in Ireland, who 'had a word with the right authorities' and the next thing John was a regular visitor to Wheatfield Prison.

On another Sunday John called me to ask if he could come to visit the church which Pam and I attended

(St. James in Crinken). He was 'taking a day off' and he would have someone with him. He duly turned up with his friend, Desmond, tagging along. It's a day we will not easily forget. That's because of the singing – not in the church, but in the local Green Dragon Well Chinese restaurant where the four of us repaired for lunch – John, Desmond, Pam and me. By way of opening the conversation, Pam and I asked, 'So, Desmond, how long have you known John?' 'Since last Tuesday.' 'Just last Tuesday! How did that happen?'

'Well, I was sitting on the footpath on Marlborough Street, my feet in the gutter really. I felt like I was finished. I had tried everything. I met Christians in Cork years ago and I joined them. They were good to me but I didn't stick with it. I crashed and burned – got back into heroin again. I thought, "I've let Jesus down – there's nowhere for me to go now." That's when John walked up and said that Jesus isn't like that – he'll always give you another chance. We bought these trousers in Penney's so I could look respectable today.'

This came out in a constant torrent. But then he dried up and meekly asked, 'Could I sing it for you? I could sing it better than talking.' 'Sure,' we said to him, while I was saying to myself, 'We're sitting in the middle of a Chinese restaurant at lunch-time on a Sunday. What will people think if our table begins to sing?!' Then I chastised myself, 'Go for broke, man – who cares what the customers think?'

In an instant, Desmond transfixed Pam and me as his beautiful tenor voice echoed through the Green Dragon Well, with a song written in 1862:

'My Jesus, I love thee, I know thou art mine;
for thee all the follies of sin I resign;
my gracious Redeemer, my Saviour art thou;
if ever I loved thee, my Jesus, 'tis now.' [24]

What the customers thought, I still don't know and don't care. We got to see into Desmond's heart. And we also saw John Eniola's vision coming true – young Irish people with a bright future who had started in the gutter.

Of course, Desmond was just one guy, but John had another card up his sleeve in his plan to educate us. He served as the PR man for the 'Redeemed Christian Church of God' a denomination that was relatively new to Ireland but well known in West Africa. They now have churches in every county in Ireland and, once a year, they hold a combined prayer meeting. John invited Pam and me to join them at that event, held in Citywest hotel in west County Dublin. We were a little curious as to why he told us, 'I'll get you good seats – in Row 2.'

We drove to the hotel in good time for the eight pm start. There were quite a lot of cars on the road that evening. We knew we were getting nearer Citywest because there were Gardai helping to keep the traffic moving. I'd never seen Guards deployed to help people get to their prayers before. Once we'd parked, we noticed

---

24 My Jesus, I love Thee, I know Thou art mine, William R. Featherston, 1862

that there was an enormous custom-built marquee on the front lawn. We found 'Row 2' – that wasn't hard. 'Row 1' in front of us was composed of journalists. But behind us, were 20,000 people well ready to pray by eight o'clock. That's why they needed the marquee. No way would they ever fit into this (or any) hotel.

The prayers were startlingly specific. For example, they prayed sincerely, by name, for God's blessing on the President and members of the government and their various families. Each batch of prayers was interspersed with hearty African hymn-singing. By two o'clock in the morning Pam and I were worn out – we're all for prayer, but our bodies have their physical limits! I heard later that the worshippers had another hour left in them.

A week later Pam and I received a kind letter from Pastor Tunde Adebayo-Oke, the leader, in Ireland, of the Redeemed Christian Church of God. He thanked us for coming and for 'bringing colour to the occasion'. It was a nice touch – somewhat tongue in cheek, of course – but it underscored a vital issue in post-secular Ireland. The majority of the fellow-Christians we had just prayed with are Irish.

The RCOG was just one of various similar networks across Ireland supporting more than 800 'independent churches' – some with members from Brazil, some from Korea, some from Romania, many with a mixture of nationalities and many contributing significantly to the life of long-since established Irish churches.

When the Romanian church 'Betania' in Mulhuddart (just off the M50 motorway in Dublin) opened their new building I went along to a service on their opening weekend. The car park was packed and the building was packed. They went to great lengths to find me a seat. I was a little late but the building seats 1200 – with room for a further 200 on the stage, along with a video wall! Almost all of the church members have fairly recently moved to Ireland. The entrepreneurial excitement of these Romanian believers was infectious.

Members of these new Christian communities, some with different colours and backgrounds, are embedded in Irish life. Many of the little kids who came with their parents to the Citywest meeting are even now growing up as potential Christian doctors, lawyers, homemakers, primary school teachers – members of our parliament even. They can be part of forming a not-so-very-secular Ireland.

CHAPTER 29

FUNDING THE FAMILY BUSINESS

Sometimes people ask me if we avoid 'talking business' on the rare times when the family can get together. The answer is, 'Absolutely not – it's the family business!' Indeed, when Myles came to distil his ideas about missionary funding into a book in 2006, he called it *Funding the Family Business.* Along with Ruth and me, he had seen our parents thrilled to bits when money *left* the family home to support people with needs greater than ours, or those that had 'sold up shop' in order to focus their lives on promoting Jesus. In the book he wrote:

'My parents were an unspectacular couple with a spectacular impact for God's kingdom…What made my parents stand out as different was their attitude to their possessions: They didn't have any. None at all. No home, no car, no food, not even any children. As far as they were concerned, they were looking after *God's* possessions. And they did it to the best of their ability, ensuring that everything that God had entrusted to their care was used to the maximum impact for God's kingdom,'[25]

Such was the appetite for this kind of information that *Funding the Family Business* is currently in a second edition in English with five print runs so far and translations including Spanish for South America, European Spanish, Romanian, German and what Myles refers to as the 'bootleg versions' in Russian and Indonesian (somebody phoned him up one day to say how helpful they had found the Russian edition – that was the first time he'd heard of it!).

The principle that Myles had noted early on – that the donor has a greater need to give than the receiver has to receive – wasn't at all original. After all, it was Jesus himself who said, 'It is more blessed to give than to receive.' It was the same principle that our parents had lived by – and Myles now spent his time opening the Bible with Christians in over 60 countries to show responsible ways of dealing with money. To enable them to do so, they found a little circle of backers who 'got it' and pledged to maintain Myles and Phyllis's own personal income so that the missionaries they visited would not be out of pocket.

I have asked Myles how on earth he answers the question when he's asked at parties, 'And what do you do?' He's got his answer down pat: 'I help local indigenous Christian charities explore how they can find resources locally without depending on external funding which can often come with unhelpful conditions.'

---

25 Funding the Family Business, Myles Wilson, Stewardship, 2006

Despite his aim to be equally helpful to a carefully curated set of prioritised cases, I bet that Myles has some pet projects, one of which surely has to be his work with Translators Association of the Philippines. From their base (in the Philippines) the chosen task of TAP is to turn the Bible from its original Hebrew and Greek into the many minority languages spoken in various Pacific-rim countries. In dealing with matters of the heart it's not quite good enough to just work through a trade language or a dominant national language.

In 2005 they asked for Myles's help to decrease their dependence on outside finance (which was unsustainable) while increasing funding from internal sources in the Philippines. Myles visited them as an adviser seven times over a few years. By that time the translators' income from Filipino churches had increased ten-fold. The first time I heard this I thought they had said ten per cent – but no, it was 1000%!

In January 2015 they sent a thank-you report to Myles in which they recorded a decade of their work to translate into Majukayong which is spoken by only a couple of thousand residents of a mountainous region of northern Luzon in the Philippines. They had just travelled through those mountains to a local ceremony to launch the brand new Majukayong New Testament. 'Our bones are still aching from the long bumpy ride, but with hearts aching with joy as well, seeing the power of God's Word to transform former head-hunters. The MC at the ceremony said, 'Now God speaks Majukayong!!!

He is no longer a white faced God.' Just hearing that kind of report keeps Myles and Phyllis going for a long time.

Myles is simply the global expert in relational fundraising in a cross-cultural context. He has travelled to every continent every year. There are only eight months in the last 29 years when he *hasn't* travelled in the cause of making missionaries' lives more liveable. Although that sounds like an admirable CV, for him it was a problem to be solved because there's only one of him.

When I met up with Myles and Phyllis recently I asked him about when he decided to solve that problem. 'When I turned sixty, I took stock of my life and decided to spend the next ten years developing four others to "take the baton" from me by the time I'm seventy. So far, I've whittled down 15 potential "baton-takers" to four.' So, for his seventieth birthday he invited the four to a 'big baton-taker hoolie'. Now there are four more 'Myleses'. The mind boggles.

In that recent conversation, while Myles was out of the room, I asked Phyllis what she would add to this story. She said, 'People often comment on Myles's wisdom. What they may not often recognise is that his wisdom is clearly earthed in the Bible. I see him when others don't, in his study poring over his Bible. And reading doesn't come easy for him because he's somewhat dyslexic – sometimes he listens to an audio version of the passage instead.'

But Myles has also had a key role to play in the wider Wilson family finances, when our parents had run the final lap of their race.

When my father retired in 1980, he and my mother moved to Newtownabbey, County Antrim. You could almost say, 'They retired, and went to hospital,' because they spent so much time there – visiting people they knew. And some people they scarcely knew, but who needed a visit. They became familiar with every hospital in the Belfast area including their parking regulations and visiting hours. In the end, it was in one of those hospitals that my father breathed his last, surrounded by family and some closest friends. By the time he was gone he had made sure that my mother was provided for and that when *she* was gone their inheritance would move in an interesting direction – not a totally secret plan, since our parents had discussed it with Myles and Ruth and me.

Some widows become withdrawn and quiet. My mother certainly did – for a while her body and mind taking their time to recover from years of caring for my father. But then she sort of woke up and realised that there was no reason she shouldn't go back to Africa to see Ruth and John who were by then in Namibia. So, she flew again. The McNeill's Namibian friends showed her the wonderful African deference accorded to older people but also they were well impressed to see this woman from Ireland climbing the famous Sossusvlei sand dunes alongside people one third of her age.

Another of Annie's ventures in this chapter of her life was painting stones. She began to collect stones about the size of her open hand and painted landscapes on them. They were mostly traditional postcard-type Irish rural settings. Sometimes they had lakes and mountains but often they had the single-storey thatched house with the two windows, so beloved of postcard publishers. One day I asked her about these little houses in her paintings. 'They're the Breesy house,' she said. 'But there's only one storey?' I enquired; 'I thought you had a two-storey house at Breesy.' 'No,' she said, 'It was like what I painted. And just two windows.' I was getting my first chance to 'see' the house where she was born and raised on that enchanting mountain. That actual house itself had, long since, collapsed into unrecognisable ruins. The place she now lived in was a small home in the northern corner of Glengormley, County Antrim.

She also kept a close eye on up-and-coming missionary candidates. Like a punter choosing horses to bet on, she would say, 'I've got a really good case of a couple going to Uruguay. Great people. They're on my list of people I'm supporting this summer.' That summer, of 2005, she had at least three such 'cases'.

One day she felt a bit woozy – nothing serious – and called the doctor. All her symptoms indicated that she had got dehydrated and could benefit from a few days of hospital care where her re-hydration could be managed well. Before she left for the Mater Hospital on the Crumlin Road in Belfast, she made very sure that her financial giving was up to date. She popped the one gift which was still outstanding into an envelope and brought it with her.

My cousin Helen Clark, who had herself been a missionary in Paraguay, accompanied her to the hospital in the non-emergency ambulance. Helen recounts the journey which was, 'a little slow because the crowds out for the Twelfth of July clogged up the street a bit. Before we got to the Mater, Annie made sure to give the ambulance driver the envelope to post.' Little did that driver know that he was holding, and then posting, the last gift to a missionary ever given by God's most secret agent in Belfast. Annie Wilson didn't last the weekend. Back in her room at home she had left the funds, a few hundred in Sterling cash, for the last four young missionaries on her list. She just hadn't got around to it. So we, in the family, sidled up individually to these four cases during my mother's funeral and handed over the final monies. As Myles recounts that occasion, 'Some of the recipients felt a bit odd.'

Myles then took on the job of sorting out our mother's tax affairs, which had a wrinkle. The British government had a system whereby any gift given to an officially recognised charity would be enhanced by the government adding any tax that the giver had already paid on this amount of income. The system by which that tax was returned was called 'Gift Aid'. Annie Wilson loved 'Gift Aid' and it loved her, or at least, the beneficiaries to whom she gave. She gave so much that we used to joke with her that she'd need to make sure she didn't go to prison for giving away more than she had received!

Of course, it's never a joke with Her Majesty's Revenue and Customs. Myles recorded the encounter in *Funding the Family Business*:

'In the midst of the grief at our sudden loss…I got a form from the tax office to complete so that my mum's tax file could be closed…It was a typical tax form and would have taken me most of a day to fill out all the information they needed. I really didn't have the time or emotional energy to spend on this, so I did a quick check and realised that almost all of the tax my Mum had paid that year had already been reclaimed through Gift Aid by the various charities she supported. There was only £7 left.

'I phoned the tax office and explained this, asking if I needed to complete the form if there was only £7 to be repaid. The person at the other end of the phone asked me to clarify this. Did I mean that my mother had given away virtually all of her taxable income? I assured him that she had given away a lot more than her taxable income, but Gift Aid had only been reclaimed on part of her giving. He'd never come across this situation before and it took a bit of convincing before he realised that I had the figures right. "Your mother must have been quite a giver," he said. "There's no need to fill in the form. I'll deem the file to be closed." '[26]

That 'sudden grief' which all of us now felt was tempered somewhat by sharing in the joy of my father's,

---

26 Funding the Family Business, Myles Wilson, Stewardship, 2006

and mother's, interesting inheritance plan. Our father had savoured the idea of at last being with the Lord in heaven while his assets helped missionaries 'in the most difficult country in the world' (difficult for missionaries, that is). So, now Myles and Ruth and I were tasked with finding a way to use the proceeds of a house in County Antrim to establish another place, somewhere in the world, where local missionaries could come and rest for a while.

Ruth and I didn't take long to agree that Myles was the best one to take the lead on this.

The money was placed in trust while the three of us scoured the world for that 'most difficult place'. Actually, finding a 'difficult country' isn't difficult – it's choosing which one! We then realised that we needed to find not just a country but an actual facility on offer and, even more important, actual people on the ground who would take on the role of hosts in such a place. He found the facility and the hosts in one of our favourite difficult countries.

All three of us flew out together to the inauguration. Ruth and I had imagined that, now that Myles was with us, we'd be able to spend the flight talking about our favourite subjects like Namibia, the Philippines, Malawi, our mother's close shave with the tax people and the Russia our parents never saw. We were going to see their new house, just like they had so often come to see ours. Their intense curiosity had led them to Malawi, Namibia, Galway, Florida, Germany, to see us, yes, and also to see what progress the kingdom of God was making there. But that cosy sibling chat on the plane was not to be!

Myles, the more seasoned traveller, already had all his gear with him for a long-haul flight sleep – face-mask, ear plugs, the lot. All that remained was for him to switch off his reading light – which wouldn't switch off. He called this to the attention of the cabin staff who explained that their only alternative was to switch off the lighting in that entire section of the plane. That was fine with Myles so, the next thing we knew, we were all in the dark!

But once we got on the ground we three felt a united surge of responsibility. We watched wide-eyed as the proceeds from a poky little bungalow in Glengormley were turned into a magnificent, generously-sized six-bedroom (en-suite) home from home for beleaguered missionaries. We met with the people who would now legally own it (it has no connection to us).

Myles, Ruth and I all said a few words of greeting to the small group that gathered. I could hardly hold it together as I tried to explain to this gathering of mostly local, mostly low-paid tradespeople that our father was not a financier. 'He was just an electrician,' I stressed, 'and our mother stayed at home to look after us and later went out to work in a factory to help support missionaries.' However much I insisted on our parents' humble origins, I could see I was wasting my time. The idea that an electrician and a factory worker could produce a house was beyond their imagination.

The property has a big garden. Maybe my fondest memory was finding that national missionary women from the locality would come and just sit in the garden for the afternoon to get a bit of peace. If Joe and Annie Wilson's lives had needed one final validation, they got it. The electrician and his wife left behind, not only a place of rest for weary Christian workers, but three children whom they had never pressurized into missionary work. The three of us, although now working on vastly different projects, still feel a bit like the three-strand hay rope that was plaited by the Myles family on Breesy mountain.

ABOUT THE AUTHOR

David Wilson was born in Strabane, County Tyrone and studied at Trinity College Dublin (Microbiology) and University College Galway (Education) and Milltown Institute Dublin (Biblical Studies).

After working in Galway and Dublin, David and his wife, Pam, have lived in Germany, Birmingham and London. From these bases they have worked in 20 different countries and led some dozens of missionary pioneers. They now make their home in Dun Laoghaire, County Dublin.

David is the author of *A New Breed of Irishmen* (1985), *Sorted* (2000) *David's Diaries* (2010) and *Sorted (Irish edition)* (2013).